Christians and Sexuality in the Time of AIDS

Christians and Sexuality in the Time of AIDS

Timothy Radcliffe, Lytta Basset, Eric Fassin

Translated by John Bowden

continuum

CONTINUUM
The Tower Building, 11 York Road, London SE1 7NX
80 Maiden Lane, Suite 704, New York, NY 10038

First published 2007

www.continuumbooks.com

Translated by John Bowden from the French *Les chrétiens et la sexualité au temps
du sida* published by Cerf.
Copyright © Cerf 2007

Translation copyright © John Bowden 2007

ISBN-13 978-08264-9911-0
ISBN-10 0826499112

British Library Cataloguing-in-Publication Data
A catalogue record for this book is available from the British Library.

Typeset by BookEns Ltd, Royston, Herts.
Printed on acid-free paper in Great Britain by MPG Books Ltd,
Bodmin, Cornwall

Contents

Foreword

James Allison

THE PRUNING AND QUICKENING OF THE
SPIRIT IN THE TIME OF AIDS

In one of those 'Do you remember what you were doing
when Kennedy was shot?' scenarios, I remember first
reading about what later became known as AIDS while
living in Mexico City in the spring of 1983. Over the
following months the medical horror quickly became
apparent, and mobilization got under way starting from
resourceful communities of gay men and their friends on
both sides of the Atlantic. However, a tectonic shift in the
cultural effect of the pandemic, at least with regards to
non-African countries, occurred in the summer of 1985.
I was visiting Nicaragua, and curiously, given the state
of the war being waged by the Reagan Administration
against the Sandinista regime, the news of Rock Hudson
being rushed for treatment to the Pasteur Institute in
Paris was carried (without explanation, for a couple of
days) in the local papers. Anyone whose antennae were
attuned to AIDS-related news, and the role of the Pasteur

Institute in research and treatment, must have guessed, as I did, what was to come: the revelation that one of the most recognizable, and charming, of the heterosexual-playing 'beaux' of the small screen had come down with AIDS. And so it was. With Rock Hudson 'outed' by his illness there began in earnest a completely unexpected and astoundingly rapid process of public discovery of worlds previously invisible to the general gaze, worlds no longer able to be comfortably placed in distant cities 'where they do things like that', but worlds coming inexorably closer to home.

It is difficult for us to remember, over 22 years later, what a difference all this has made in terms of what can be and can't be talked about. For along with the fear and the shame and all the other emotions generated by the advance of the pandemic, there also developed a need to describe things previously left passed over. Not because prurience became fashionable, but because accurate ways of describing methods for preventing contagion became necessary. And along with these, more accurate accounts of the workings of human anatomies and sexual practices than had been widespread became commonplace. Furthermore, as it became urgent to understand the virus's epidemiology, so the sociology of human behavioural patterns suddenly had to become much more aware of what actually was the case concerning the sexual lives of human beings, in contradistinction both to publicly upheld social norms, and to the self-reporting of individuals within our societies.

Not only, however, in contradistinction to those norms and to that self-reporting: also in sensitive partnership with them. It quickly became clear that applying what was, in the eyes of many societies, a white Anglo-Saxon term, 'gay', to groupings where no one could identify with the word, would not help prevent transmission of anything, nor encourage any sort of responsibility of conduct. So it became necessary to find quite other ways of talking: about 'men who have sex with men' for instance (it being understood that these are primarily married, family men with children). And so, with all its ups and downs, the sheer complexity of real human life and its sexual, emotional, financial, familial and para-familial kinship creation structures became more visible to studious eyes than it had been, at least in the West, since the onset of modernity's attempts to prune the riotous efflorescence of human togetherness into rational and decorous hedgerows.

Of course, it was not the advent of AIDS which kick-started this process, nor was it even the most significant factor in it. The unrelated, but almost simultaneous, dawning of awareness of the extent to which the sexual abuse of children is prevalent in all our societies, and of quite how much of that abuse is incestuous, is another symptom of the same process. It too has been a major source of the new visibility of all our own social realities, and of our need to be reflective about them, which has come to permeate our picture of ourselves. However there seems little doubt that the advent of AIDS speeded up this process, and has forced upon us certain lenses through which to make sense of it. Where would the impetus for some sort of civil recognition for long-term relationships other than traditional marriage, which is now a normal part of the cultural and political process of all western countries, have come from, had it not been for the frequent and grotesque inequities meted out by either, or all of, 'families', hospitals and state bureaucracies to the surviving partner of a same-sex couple whose other half had died of AIDS?

This is the context within which it is my honour to introduce *Christians and Sexuality in the Time of AIDS* to you. The reflections on which you are about to embark are the fruit of a colloquium which took place in Paris in January 2006 organized by the ecumenical group *Chrétiens et Sida*. The group was formed in 1990 as part of a Church-related response to the world whose parameters were becoming visible as AIDS advanced in the francophone countries. All of the authors of the pages which follow are from that francophone world, with the exception of Timothy Radcliffe, whose participation in the colloquium is a sign of his honorary francophone status: he studied in Paris, is a frequent visitor to, and speaker at, French cultural and theological events, and is an even better-selling author in France than he is in his native England.

So why introduce the fruit of a francophone colloquium of this sort to an English readership? 'Have we not enough distinguished commentators of our own in this field for a collection of this sort to be "de trop"?', you may say. Well, I would ask you to reconsider this opinion because I think it is worth listening to a slightly different approach to many of the issues which we typically deal with in other ways. Our Anglophone discussions have tended to be about practicalities, and the morality involved in decision making. Where the issue of Christian response to the world opening up 'in the time of AIDS' is discussed, it tends to follow our English-speaking culture's somewhat infantile attitudes towards the Vatican's approach to the matter at hand. And I mean infantile in two senses: infantile conspiracy-theory attributions of 'genocide' to the Vatican's stance on condoms, and corresponding assumptions about how 'powerful' any Vatican position is in its hold over the conscience of the Catholic faithful (assumptions which owe more to secularized versions of Reformation polemic than to any grasp of reality) on the one hand; and infantile on the other hand, since, when clearly ridiculous moral postures are put forward by Vatican officials, their absurdity is compounded by ideological defenses made by people who seem no more capable of a nuanced reading of what it means to be 'Church' than their evangelical counterparts are capable of a nuanced reading of what it means to have a 'Bible'.

For instance, no one could be Pope and yet not maintain, at least when put on the spot by public events, the current magisterial positions to the best of his ability. Not to do so would quickly lead to his removal from the job. The really interesting questions surrounding what a Pope is doing are never the politically immediate headline grabbers, but always the small, apparently insignificant tinkerings round the edges which are either going to make change possible over time, or try to block it. Seen in this perspective, the notion that Pope Benedict is as absolutist as his predecessor, or for instance, as homophobic, seems to me the result of a serious misreading of how anybody could possibly undertake modest change-management in that job. Benedict's quiet maintenance of the status quo while gently undoing some of the screws that hold some of the sillier positions in place, just beneath the surface of what hits the public gaze, seems to me wholly admirable.

The media picked up, for instance, that under Pope Benedict, the Church has dropped its teaching on Limbo. But how many picked up on the officially approved understanding of how Church teaching can develop, an understanding which is in principle also true in other spheres, which is apparent in the relevant document? I certainly didn't until it was pointed out to me! Everyone has picked up that the Pope is opposed to proposals for same-sex (and indeed other-sex) civil unions in Italy. But how many picked up that where the Italian Bishops Conference has weighed in particularly on the issue of the gender of the partners, the Pope has concentrated much more strongly on the question of permanence, on the 'till death do us part' nature of the loving relationship that is marriage, as opposed to the more temporary forms of union being proposed. It is this indispensable permanence that he doesn't want to see sold down the river, because to do so would diminish the demands of, and the expectations of the human capacity for, love. Something that future generations may well be able to pick up when the issue of the genders involved is not such a hot potato.

So, welcome to a slightly different world: one where immediate moral disputes take second place to explorations of something rather more subtle. I would like to offer you, from outside the text you are embarking on, two guidelines for reading this rather more subtle reality. The first is from Papa Ratzinger, in recent spontaneous remarks to a group of priests who met with him towards the end of his July 2007 summer holiday in the Dolomites, when he was asked to comment on how he saw the Church developing since the Second Vatican Council. He refers to the great clashes that developed in the wake of the Council, and which seem to have dominated the life of the Church since then:

> In this – let us say – serious, great clash between the new, healthy modernity desired by the Council and the crisis of modernity, everything becomes difficult, like after the first Council of Nicaea.
>
> One side was of the opinion that this cultural revolution was what the Council had wanted. It identified this new Marxist cultural revolution with the will of the Council. It said: This is the Council; in the letter the texts are still a bit antiquated, but behind the written words is this 'spirit,' this is the will of the Council, this is what we must do. And on the other side, naturally, was the reaction: you are destroying the Church. The – let us say – absolute reaction against the Council, anticonciliarity, and – let us say – the timid, humble search to realize the true spirit of the Council. And as a proverb says: 'If a tree falls it makes a lot of noise, but if a forest grows no one hears a thing,' during these great noises of mistaken progressivism and absolute anticonciliarism, there grew very quietly, with much suffering and with many losses in its

construction, a new cultural passageway, the way
of the Church.[1]

Pope Benedict seems well aware that over the last 40
years a new, rather quiet and not easily identified reality
– 'a new cultural passageway' – is growing up. This is a
way of being Church which cannot be identified either
with an aggressively secularist reading of modernity,
nor with a religiously based refusal to face up to it, but
requires working through a great number of realities,
slowly, patiently and without arrogance.

My second guideline is taken from the philosopher-
historian Rémi Brague, one of the most distinguished of
contemporary French Catholic intellectuals. His book *La Loi
de Dieu*[2] examines the similarities and differences between the
historical ways in which each of the three great monotheistic
religious cultures, the Jewish, the Islamic and the Christian,
handles the concept of Law in relation to God. One of
his points is that in Christianity, unlike in the other two
monotheistic cultures, the concept of 'divine law' has from
the outset occupied a curiously non-essential, secondary and
indeed waning place. Brague reminds us that:

Our societies, with their programme of a legal
system pruned of divine associations, have in fact

---

[1] From Matthew Sherry's translation of the exchange on http://chiesa.
espresso.repubblica.it/dettaglio.jsp?id=158061&eng=y
For the original Italian: www.vatican.va/holy_father/benedict_xvi/
speeches/2007/july/documents/hf_ben-xvi_spe_20070724_clero-ca-
dore_it.html
[2] Paris: Gallimard 2005

been made possible in the final analysis by the Christian experience of a divinity pruned of legal associations ... The would-be struggles for the 'laicisation' of institutions are rushing to the aid of a victory acquired centuries ago, and which is the very victory of Christianity in its most official form: that of the Church establishing for itself the limits which separate it from the secular sphere.

Once the divine presence has ceased to be conceived of, and undergone, as if it were a law, there is no less of a question to be raised concerning how what is of God genuinely should be articulated with our practice. We have no proof that the understanding of politics which is proper to the West is a strong one, or indeed one viable in the long term. That human activity can, without reference to God, develop itself freely, rather than drown itself in suicidal dialectics: this is what has yet to be shown. And it may well be that it is as the idea of a divine law grows distant that this question can be set free into being asked in such a way that what is most burning in it becomes clear.[3]

In other words: the gradual collapse of an extrinsic divine basis for legal normativity is not something contrary to Christianity, but is part of what Christianity is about. This means that contemporary unease about religious language being expressed in terms of legal normativity, and the contemporary search for a proper understanding

---

[3] op.cit. p. 315 my translation.

of legal normativity which has a basis which is both immanent, intrinsic to the human condition, and yet universally true and non-relativistic, this is something which is not the sign of a collapse of the Christian faith. Rather, given that there is nothing anti-nomian in this, nor does it advocate a descent into an ethics that is merely situational, we are very close to the centre of what we would expect to be happening in our societies, given the truth of the Christian faith.

And here I think Ratzinger and Brague are at one: the 'new cultural passageway' and Brague's burning question as to how, with the waning of law as a useful concept for undergoing God, we are to articulate the relationship between God and how we are to behave, seem to me to have much in common.

In different ways, each of the contributors to this colloquium is inside this tentative creation of a new and non-arrogant cultural passageway. Their parameters are formed not only by the world which has become visible in the time of AIDS, but by the twin challenges of recognizing the loss of credibility of a religious teaching based on collapsing notions of normativity, and yet also recognizing the importance of discovering, and helping to make strong and viable emerging forms of normativity which lead to flourishing. This, I think, is what underlies Eric Fassin's fascinating discussion of what he calls the 'democratization' of language, which is not at all the same thing as a call for the 'democratization' of the Church – indeed, it may turn out to be the only healthy basis for a properly servant form of hierarchical life in the midst of the Church. It is also what marks Timothy

Radcliffe's passion for making a new and Eucharistic language of bodily generosity and fidelity available as the basis for understanding sexual ethics. This is not at all the same thing as simply ditching previously held sexual ethics. It is rather the realization that it is only a new framework of meaning, discovered from within by its participants, which will bring out and keep alive all that was good and holy about previous paradigms of understanding.

For my own part, what strikes me about this process of the painful reconfiguring of what it means to be Christian in the world which has been opening up to us, and forcing us to open up to it, is how it is marked by the Holy Spirit. If, as Brague has pointed out, we find the notion of 'law' an increasingly unhelpful one with which to imagine God's dealing with us, then the obvious question becomes one of the shape of the Spirit in our lives. And here I would like to leave you with some tentative remarks of my own which will, I hope, help to frame what you are about to read.

It is part of what is essential to Trinitarian monotheism that it sets us free from gods. This means in practice that as each dimension of who God is becomes clearer, so it also becomes clearer what is not God, but a god. And along with that, as the sky is cleared of gods, so we become both freer, and more aware of our responsibility.

Thus it was the emergence among the Hebrews of God who is not one of the Gods which led to the astounding discovery we call Creation. This is the realization that there is an 'outside' to everything that is, and therefore that everything that is is contingent, available to reason and responsibility, and not run by weird forces and projections.

Thus it was too that the emergence of God's High Priest as a crucified criminal put to death by the religious and political authorities of the time made available for us the complete non-sacrality of any human religious or political system. In other words, there is an 'outside' to human anthropology and sociology, such that we become capable of undoing our own socialized lies and self-deception, and thus become able to understand what is really 'there' in a way which is not simply a marker established by the victory of the powerful in any given conflict, but is stronger than any such relativism.

And because what was breathed on us from on high wasn't a law, but was Spirit, the very shape and strength of the Creator's desire, we have gradually found ourselves coming to see that there is an 'outside' to human desire. This means that we find ourselves able to discover what is true about human desire, how it works, how it fails, without feeling we are trapped in something sacred, something frightening. Part of what we would expect to collapse as a result of the Creator being known among us as Spirit, and not as Law, is the dichotomy between sacred desire and impure desire. Gradually there is unfolding to us the way in which a holy desire can emerge which is not the same as something corresponding to human taboos, but which starts where we are and recreates us without displacing us.

I suspect that the advent of psychology, and of the huge increase in people searching for spiritual retreats, are part of this process of our learning that there is an 'outside' to human desire, made available in our midst by God's Desire. And I also suspect that this is one of the reasons why, over the last 40 years or so, the quite modern perception that church authority is all about control of sex has become so prevalent, both in the detractors of the Church and in its defenders. It could scarcely be otherwise if what we are undergoing is the period when the Spirit is showing us at a more and more popularly widespread level what it means that there is an 'outside' to human desire, that we can know things about it objectively, and that the language of extrinsically-derived normativity which was part of our protection from knowing too much about ourselves is a declining taboo as we come to develop richer and more realistic pictures of human flourishing. Ones which are undergoing the pruning and quickening which is the work of the Spirit.

The texts upon which you are about to embark tell us, as does so much else, that the Holy Spirit has not been absent, nor its work fruitless, in the time of AIDS.

James Alison
Umbria, London July/August 2007

Introduction: Why This Book?

Jean-Louis Vildé

Like any epidemic, AIDS not only causes suffering to patients, but disrupts every institution. However, it also has a special character, resulting from its modes of transmission: it affects everyone intimately, particularly in their sexuality. It seems to us important that Christians, who from the beginning have been made sensitive to the questions raised by AIDS, are again paying attention to them twenty-five years after the appearance of this illness.

Our 'Christians & AIDS' organization was created in 1990 by Antoine Lion and some other pioneers, with the aim of not leaving Christians and their church institutions out of the fight against the illness and helping them to become aware of the ethical, social and religious issues connected with this epidemic.

Without being indebted or affiliated to church institutions, we maintain fraternal and natural relations with them. So we share with our churches and the other associations which are fighting AIDS the solidarity with patients that is needed, the struggle against discrimination and the exclusion of victims of AIDS by our societies and sometimes even by those around them. There are no good sicknesses and bad sicknesses. We also adopt the Christian values which give a positive meaning to sexuality in all its multiple facets: the joy of meeting, procreation, stable commitment and respect for the body along with desire, pleasure and the celebration of the body. But it is true that we are often, to different degrees, dissatisfied with the responses of the churches to the questions raised by the epidemic. All too often what they say, which bears witness to a mistrust of sexuality, has been badly received by the faithful, who have then kept their distance. In conformity to our charter we try to help our churches to reflect, to speak, to prompt debates, to avoid attitudes which are too brusque or standpoints which are sometimes misrepresented and often badly understood. With them we try to make Christians aware of the gravity of this epidemic, reminding them of the solidarity which is needed with the poorest, the most deprived, the rejects of society, all those who have been wounded by life.

More than ten years after the announcement of the discovery of new antiretroviral treatments on 31 January 1996, the epidemic continues among young homosexuals, immigrants to Europe, and even more in the Third World, especially in Africa. It is then that questions of prevention arise which provoke debates, confrontations, conflicts, sometimes even anathemas on one side or the other. However, it has to be remembered that in this struggle all means which can prevent the transmission of the disease must be considered, even if they relate to different spheres; all men and women must protect the freedom of their consciences and responsibility for their behaviour and the choice of a means of prevention.

How do we relate to one another the three human dimensions of the body with its failings, its drives (including sexual drives) and its pleasures; the cerebral, with thought, affectivity, the relational life, desire; and finally the transcendent, the religious, the divine? The ancient Greeks had already found a link: the visitor to Delphi could see brought together for the first time in the same magnificent place, at the geographical centre of Greece, the stadium, the theatre and the temple, uniting these three essential components of every human person.

But let's return to the theme of this book, to the questions raised by the three words 'Christians', 'sexuality' and 'AIDS'. Sometime they are difficult to associate, even just two of them. We see the texts which come next as an occasion for deepening our reflections and following the debate on these questions: they do not necessarily provide definitive replies but perhaps they open up new paths. Here, alongside theological and sociological discussions, you will find testimonies to the reality of the suffering caused by this epidemic and standpoints which reflect the experience of the members of our association. Here is a confrontation between testimonies or reflections drawn from the experience of those in contact with the sick and those close to them, and developed analyses which originate in a more general reflection on questions posed by theology and the social sciences. This is essential, even if the link between the two approaches does not seem to be a direct one. It allows those who are active to take the general reflections on board more easily and to benefit from them in their everyday activities.

The first part of the book, then, contains texts commissioned by our association on three major questions and testimonies recalling the background of tribulations against which this adventure unfolds. The second part puts forward three analyses based on theology or the human sciences. Eric Fassin, who teaches sociology at the École normale supérieure in Paris, analyses the foundations of what he calls 'a sexual democracy'. Lytta Basset, from Lausanne, a pastor and psychoanalyst, re-reads the biblical narrative of the creation of man and woman in order to rethink the relationship between members of a couple, of whatever kind. The Dominican, Timothy Radcliffe, from Oxford, former Master of the Order of Preachers, presents the main lines of a 'Christian sexual ethic' which he discerns in the gospel of the Eucharist. In Part Three a broad discussion takes these texts further. Before a conclusion by Antoine Lion, as an overture you can read the reaction of an African, Abdon Goudjo, to this work, which has chosen to limit itself to the framework of Western culture. It is good to allow ourselves to be questioned, perhaps disturbed, by a voice coming from what is the most sorely tried continent.

We should not forget that one of our basic virtues is that of hope. Let us share it with all those who are confronted with this sickness, with those who will read this book, and go on working out replies to the difficult questions which AIDS continues to raise, so that the Christian message remains audible, even in this period of suffering and doubt.

Part One

Openings

Chapter 1

Positions and Questions: 'Christians & AIDS'

NOT JUDGING

As has often been said and written, the AIDS epidemic has been a revelation about the behaviour of men and women in the sphere of their private lives.

At the beginning of the 1980s, carers saw young men arriving in hospitals, often in good health, who had been discovered to be carriers of a virus heralding an apparently unavoidable premature death. Three sets of feelings emerged among these young people: fear, anger and above all shame. Shame, for one of the first questions to be answered for the consultant's medical file was 'How were you contaminated?' This was not a matter of curiosity, but a legal obligation, in order to focus the orientation of prevention campaigns. Even if in thirteen per cent of cases the response was 'I don't know', this intrusion into people's personal life was felt to be intolerable. Hence the shame, because to say that one was HIV positive conjured up the kind of intimacy found

3

in the statistics: sexual promiscuity, homosexuality, the use of drugs . . . There was also and above all the feeling of being judged to be a delinquent with a single glance.

But how can one refrain from making a judgement when confronted with irresponsible behaviour which puts lives in danger? How, for example, can one condemn the passing on of contaminated syringes which make the epidemic flare up without taking the pathology of a dependence on illicit products into account? It was years before a ministry of health decided to implement a real policy of reducing risks, allowing drug users to inject themselves properly and offering substitute treatments for heroin addicts. For thirty years in France, for example, a single thought held sway: 'Drugs mustn't be given to drug addicts; that would make them dependent on social medicine. Pharmacists shouldn't sell them syringes; that would condone their vice.' Faced with the spread of HIV contamination, we have had to change the way we look at those who have been treated as delinquents, who have been accused of all kinds of evil without being offered any help. Since this change, made on the insistence of certain psychiatrists and people active in the field, heroin addicts no longer contaminate themselves with syringes. This realistic and beneficial attitude wasn't easy to implement; there was strong resistance. The important thing was to instil trust, not to judge, to understand what people were experiencing, to let them speak, and finally to listen to them. Such an ethic isn't reserved for Christians.

To act in this way rules out all the processes of stigmatization and exclusion which scorn rights and dignity, overburdening the existence of so many infected people. Stigmatization used to be a practice of marking slaves or the condemned with a red-hot iron. Today, to feel stigmatized is to tell oneself 'I'm an addict', 'I'm a whore', thus integrating the negative discourse of the other as a personal truth.

A survey made by the AIDS Information Service in 2005 was interested in 'actions and reflections on discrimination'. It established that:

- 6 out of 10 HIV positive persons said that they had been discriminated against by this fact;
- The medical sphere is the first domain of discrimination in social life: the dentist who thinks it useless to invest in dentures 'given the short time the patient has to live'; the gynaecologist who decides to remove the uterus for a simple fibroid once he learns that the patient is HIV positive. Such attitudes can also be found in the spheres of insurance, of banks which refuse credit, etc.;
- There is discrimination in both private life and social life: family, friends, partners, all those active in everyday life are concerned.

The result is that a number of people no longer disclose that they are HIV positive; to protect themselves, they count themselves out and marginalize themselves – and that is how the epidemic grows in the world. This opting out is steadily increasing: the page would be full to overflowing if one added to all the causes of stigmatization linked to AIDS those which originate in poverty, skin colour, the fact of being a foreigner. What have we done that, after twenty years of messages about prevention in which we have given priority to information, offered the young and not so young the means of exercising their responsibility and accepting their choices, there is still this feeling of fear and rejection?

The gospel tells Christians that Christ did not hesitate to judge his disciples severely: 'I was hungry and you gave me no food, I was in prison and you did not visit me.' Little by little they understand the meaning of these reproaches. However, Jesus does not condemn them but makes them aware: 'What you did to the smallest of these you did to me.' We must engage in dialogue in the trust which makes people grow, instead of constantly condemning them.

That leads us to question a classical solution to the contradiction between the gospel which does not judge and the reminder of moral norms: it is said that we must judge conduct, not people. Now according to one of us: 'Good health and self-esteem are needed if I am not to feel judged by someone who judges my behaviour.' It is impossible to keep to 'I condemn the acts and respect those who commit them.' There are situations in which one can only express oneself by actions. How can one ask homosexuals to express themselves sexually otherwise than by homosexual relations?

In that case don't we risk forgetting responsibility? No, for if sexuality is part of the private sphere, it includes social involvement. The basic duty to protect oneself and others, which is constantly recalled in the framework of prevention, is addressed to all, young or adult, HIV positive or HIV negative. So it is a matter of welcoming the sick person unconditionally, without judging the past, and recalling the law, the demand for respect of persons when it comes to prevention and, more broadly, in all sexual practices.

'Where does evil come from?' asked the philosopher and sociologist Edgar Morin. 'Partly from the cruelty of the world, and partly from human ignorance,' he replied. 'The Greeks said that the bad person is ignorant . . . We need to regenerate the sources of ethics and regenerate ourselves from them: these sources are solidarity and responsibility.'

IMBALANCE: CHURCH MORALITY AND PERSONAL MORALITY

A major theological tradition believes that a rule which is made by the church's magisterium but rejected by the Christian people loses its legitimacy. That raises the problem of the relationship between the message of the gospel, the rule pronounced and the practices of the faithful. This question concerns all the Christian churches and also the members of 'Christians & AIDS' who sometimes experience a conflict between their personal convictions based on a Christian point of reference and certain rules favoured by the churches. It is from this experience that we raise the question of the origin, the content and the justification of these rules.

The members of the association are not unanimous. Our debates throw up many questions about sexual morality outside the shared certainties, based on experience of living with the disease and our preventative actions.

7

Beyond our evident respect for the model of the stable, long-term, healthy and lasting heterosexual couple, what we reject is the deprecation and condemnation of any other way of expressing sexuality, homosexuality in particular. In fact for Christians, as for the whole of our society, AIDS has brought about a sharper awareness of the variety of ways in which sexuality (or sexualities) is (are) expressed. The message of the gospel leads us to think that the churches have more to say than a uniform condemnation. For example, how can the church, which utters fine words at the funerals of those who have died of AIDS, also utter them to those living with the virus?

These debates have shown that the words and actions of Jesus himself constitute our major point of reference; the First Testament and some writings of Paul and the church fathers often cause difficulties. Many prescriptions about sexuality seem obsolete today, even if Jesus came to 'fulfil' the law and not to abolish it.

What can the word of a church, any church, base itself on in relation to sexuality and morality more generally if the references of scripture have to be subject to reinterpretation, and if the Catholic reference to the natural law, thought to be untouchable, no longer seems to command obedience? It seems possible to agree on the fact that morality consists in appealing to responsibility, allowing persons to choose the means. This position relates to the role of the churches in education for responsibility, their function of 'illuminating consciences'. It remains to discover how this is to be done in practice.

LOVE AND SEXUALITY

For the majority of the members of 'Christians & AIDS' sexuality is bound up above all with love, and in our culture Christianity has fully strengthened this link. That can raise a problem for some of our partners in the struggle against AIDS, and even among Christians. Everywhere humanity seeks to 'dress up' the sexual drive, and this decoration shows the difference between human beings and animals. Love then presents itself as a humanization of sexuality. But is it the only possibility, or are there others?

The practice of prevention leads us first to recall the primordial rule, 'Thou shalt not kill', and thus to reject all forms of violence, in particular the violence which consists in risking contaminating one's partner. On that point there is unanimity among us. More difficult to open up, and not always clearly presented, is the debate on sexuality from which love is absent and in which there is only the quest for pleasure. Isn't there a possibility that values such as shared desire, respect for the other, sincerity, manifest themselves here? And mustn't we recall even more strongly the principle of not judging when confronted with certain forms of sexual life?

A reply to these questions can be found in the conviction that in every situation there is a way of progress and a way of regression. We must refuse to judge anyone by acts alone. The important thing is what goes on in the heart.

Discussions in schools present us with these questions. Sex education at school – for everyone, not specifically for Christians – cannot be restricted to the physical level.

It is also an education in relationships, in love, bringing in the problem of time, taking the long term into account as opposed to the drive involved in sexual desire. But what sex education should be promoted in practice? How far can one go in this domain? What values are we to transmit to pupils who have no Christian points of reference? And how?

Chapter 2

A Time of Trial: Testimonies

'In the time of AIDS' . . . This time is not just a chronological marker; it is a time of trial and sufferings. Some remarks by various men and women who have been smitten by the epidemic are a powerful reminder of these afflictions.

'Living with AIDS, with the fear of transmitting it, with the fear of being contaminated, with failing strength, with a body that one no longer recognizes, with the terrible sensation of no longer being lovable, of no longer being loved, of no longer loving oneself . . .'

People live with AIDS, perhaps for many months, for many years, knowing that it will get worse at some point. As we confront the unacceptable, the inability of present-day science to conquer the virus, even if it makes it possible to relieve the sick, we are tempted to turn towards irrational explanations: it is God's punishment, indeed, it is a grace. We must reaffirm very strongly that neither punishment nor grace are acceptable answers, even if there is a great temptation to take them as such. The response is not in heaven, but here and now.

What gives value to life, what gives it savour, is the relationship between one individual and another, the riches of personal encounter, the brotherly or sisterly way in which we look at someone else and accept the way in which he or she looks at us. With AIDS, our responsibility is to allow each person to be loved and to say 'I love you' to the end, for as long as they are capable of doing so, in a word, to live and to enjoy life. Then, only then, can the words of the Song of Songs echo in us: 'Love is as strong as death.' Then we will be able to say, like the disciples on the Emmaus road at the breaking of the bread, 'Did not our hearts burn within us when he spoke to us on the way?'

'I'm thirty-eight. I've known Philip for about fifteen years. He told me immediately that he was HIV positive. In the first years the question of having a child together couldn't arise, as there was no way of preventing contamination from the sperm of an HIV-positive man. During those years, sometimes I had a very strong desire for a child, though I couldn't contemplate it with him. He loved children so much that he was ready to adopt one. So the problem at that time was put on hold.

In 2000, scientists discovered a method of inseminating in the uterus sperm which had been treated beforehand. We had to wait until 2002 for our file to reach the hospital concerned. From that time on we paid numerous visits for inseminations, all of which failed, and then for fertilization with the injection of ova, a method which was thought to be more effective; however, that too failed. Sometimes I had to spend a couple of weeks at the hospital. Philip usually accompanied me. I was forced to stop work for illness, and that caused problems. We met couples there who had the same problem, or others, with procreation. These attempts and failures led to various obsessions.

We decided to stop attempts at fertilization for a while, to marry and to devote ourselves to buying a house. Now we have one, and we're enjoying it. This purchase gave us strength as a couple, to the point that I can now contemplate new attempts more serenely, and risk new failures. Soon we're going to resume a programme of assisted fertilization.

In the end of the day, while I have a strong desire for a child, I believe that the solidity of our marriage is more important. Certainly I know that Philip has the illness, it's part of our story, but we find strength in our marriage to live, for the present and for the future.'

'Letter to my mother and my little sister.

Seven years. Seven, a number which is said to be magical and beneficial. Seven years, the length of my cowardly solitary silence, of my time as a patient without symptoms, of my cohabitation with the virus, of questions and doubts. Seven years without a word on this aspect of my life to you, mother, or to you, Karine, for fear of disturbing you, of unfairly alarming you, of acting selfishly. I'm fine, don't worry. I'm fine despite the treatment that I've been undergoing for two years. There are people who are sicker than I am, there are illnesses which are more unfair, public opinion is improving, there are hopes of tolerance and support, of progress.

I contracted the virus because I wanted to love; because I love differently, because I was young, naïve; because homosexuality makes one unstable. Homosexuals cannot love in broad daylight, with trust and respect for the other. However, I have always aimed to live faithfully, simply, with a friend. Failing that, one has to become used to solitude and ephemeral loves.

Seven years with this handicap, an obstacle to making firm plans, to the future. Seven years. But I don't know, I no longer know how to talk about myself, my body, my desires. The failings of childhood and adolescence grow stronger. Unconsciously, perhaps I have to live like my father, shut up in my secrets, a victim of my reserve.

Seven years, and I'm going to be thirty, always too fearful, indecisive about essential actions, with a thirst for friendship, for love, for words, for bravery and constancy. Seven years with this additional label: homosexual, a teacher who has overstepped the mark, HIV positive with a medical experience which is growing. Hospital corridors anxiously paced up and down in uncertainty, monthly blood tests, waiting for the results, never too good, never too bad.

But I'm fine and I love you.

I'm fine, and I say to Katrine, "Take care when you love, love faithfully and with a conscience."'

'Phil is dying of AIDS. In a room in the hospital his wife, his parents, his friends are sharing in his death. The atmosphere is transparent. It's everyday life with a little more of eternity.

And has no one spoken of God? . . . For a long time

I've suppressed my religious practices, which I thought indispensable in such circumstances. My faith has been cleansed and I've thought about God and Jesus Christ, outside my church, calmly and gently: the scales have fallen from my eyes and I've seen and heard men and women who by instinct have lived out the Beatitudes truthfully.

Phil was brave. He had fought so hard that we had believed that he was indestructible. Now we watch, powerless, this prodigious struggle between human being and creator which inevitably involves the utmost solitude. And Phil kept struggling, for his friends, for his wife, for himself . . . up to the moment when he received the right to experience his dying. Then he became relaxed, pacified. It was as if by a miracle he was spared the suffering of the last moment. Without a groan or a convulsion, he left . . . for another place.

The silence wasn't oppressive and time went on and on . . . Someone there said, "He's like Christ", another "It's three in the afternoon", yet another, "He's thirty-three." That's all. It was the eve of the Feast of the Transfiguration.

The day went by as it were with muffled tread. It was as if, like little ants, we were going round and round a great mystery, an infinite reality which both frightened us and attracted us. Phil was a brave man, simple and invincible. But what is courage, if one doesn't feel loved? Friendship, the love of those close to him, transcended him and allowed him to experience his dying to the full. In the end, it doesn't matter in whose name we can love . . . The essential thing is to love.'

'I'm sixty-four, a grandfather, I've been an active member of "Christians & AIDS" for nine years. I won't speak of my adolescence, but of what followed, my life as a married man.

I left my wife in 1987. I quickly saw that once again I was sexually attracted to men. This was the time of harsh and murderous AIDS. Up to that point I had been protected by fidelity to my family. Shedding shame and guilt, I started to meet many men, picking them up in the street or on sex chat-lines. I was forty-six, and it seemed to me that I was compensating for my teenage years and a youth during which my sexuality didn't blossom. Prevention was difficult and I often reached a dead end. In the sexual act it is difficult to keep one's resolutions and control one's behaviour. I hasten to say that when chatting people up, in person or on the telephone, one doesn't necessarily fail to respect the other. I've found relationships and friendships there which have lasted for years. I've even written a prayer that got published, saying that God can be present in what are called places of debauchery.

In 1989 I met Michael through a chatline. We were unable to see each other for several weeks but we soon established a very strong relationship, to the point that he left his wife and got a divorce to live with me. Our relationship was a tender one. AIDS was no longer a danger for the two of us. Our sexual life soon became one of complete abstinence. Michael had cancer of the bladder and the kidneys. After several major operations and two years of dialysis, he died in 1994.

In the meantime we had discovered the "David and Jonathan" association which brings together homosexual and Christian men and women. That did us a lot of good. AIDS struck cruelly and solidarity was strong. After Michael went, I resumed my sexual wanderings, but no longer looked for a lasting relationship. It was always difficult to take no risks. I fought more strongly at "David and Jonathan" and took part in a project against AIDS called "Hope 2000". I thought that serving in an association aimed at prevention would help me here. I tried to explain my difficulties in taking precautions, but the association wasn't yet ready to listen, only to prescribe. Then I came across the "Christians & AIDS" group which knew about listening to my difficulties and supporting me.

Then, again on a chatline, I met Gabriel, who had AIDS. He was looking for "friendship and love". When we met he told me his HIV status. There again, I felt protected. We didn't have sexual relations as his libido had disappeared. But I was faithful and abstinent. That seemed to me to come automatically, and it isn't difficult when one loves and lives as a couple. Gabriel kept up his treatment in an exemplary way. He died of a heart attack after four years.

At the moment I have a friend. We get on together marvellously well. We see each other often but don't truly live as a couple, something that I regret. I compensate by a sexual life with some friends in which the relationship between us is only one of play and pleasure, but with respect for one another. We observe the rules of reciprocal protection. Even if protection has become an absolute rule for me, I know that I have to be vigilant, since the occasion can always arise of allowing myself to be carried away, forgetting how precious the person before me is and how I am responsible for him.'

'In January 1998 I underwent a test because I had doubts about the health of my friend, whom I had known for three years. The test proved positive, and the doctor who saw me told me the result brutally. Immediately I was afraid and thought of death. I sorted out my affairs and cleared everything up. I had feelings of hatred. It was as if I had been deceived, rather like a rape. I was depressed and I couldn't talk about it to anyone. However, I had to make a show of strength to my son and my mother who were living with me. I got thinner, and when people asked me about this I told them that I was on a diet. After eighteen months I decided to tell my brother, who was very friendly, and I felt better morally. Then I was able to talk about it to my son, who was very understanding, but I could never tell my mother.

I knew of the existence of an association where the sick could meet, but I didn't dare to go since I had the impression that it wasn't for women. I went all the same. I'm not the only one, but it seems to me that men and women who are sick don't talk of AIDS in the same way. The women talk about their treatments, their health worries; the men talk more about sex. It's very hard for a woman to have this illness. When one is single, as I am, one gets the impression that one is considered an easy woman who has lovers.

I've looked after myself since I discovered I was HIV positive. I'm in tritherapy. An illness linked with AIDS is something of a handicap. For me the most difficult, the most terrible thing, is to have to hide my sickness, but the essential thing is to keep hoping at any price.'

'I feel judged. A while ago a priest invited me for a meal, but sadly this dimension of brotherliness, sharing and welcome is an exception. I very rarely find a priest I feel I can speak to, for fear of being judged. Faced with the constraints of the church's ideology I feel a great emptiness at the level of personal relations. I feel useless and idle, and this leads me to fill this void with sex-shop-type excesses.

Since AIDS entered my life I have felt more respect for others. One can use a person like a Kleenex, but knowing that I risk contaminating him, I give pride of place to his intrinsic value. There is more than personal pleasure in a relationship. With sexuality it is difficult to see what my behaviour implies in the inner life of the other. Is God beyond morality?

Having lived a life of abstinence for three months in order to try to reconcile myself with God, I was surprised to be given, just afterwards, some catastrophic test results. And I was waiting for a sign! I realize that life isn't a matter of quid pro quos, but that God wants me to transform myself in depth, that this corresponds to the reality of my inner being and not to an effort of will.

As the philosopher Gustave Thibon says (and I'm quoting him from memory): "You will be amazed to see how good and evil are linked: for there are virtues which lead to loss and faults which can save."'

'It's very difficult for me even today to speak of my son who died seven years ago. The grief is still there, deep within my heart. Sometimes it makes me speak of my "little one", but the memory of his disappearance is so painful.

My young son left home in good health at the age of twenty-one, to work in a big city. Very soon afterwards, when I was in a convalescent home for health problems, he told me by telephone that he had a man friend, that he was homosexual. I was shaken, astounded, but I could tell him despite my emotions that I wanted him to be happy, that what counted for me was his happiness.

Then three years went by. One day I received a call from his friend telling me that my child was living his last moments in hospital, because of AIDS. I didn't stop to think but rushed to his bedside. My son died the next day.

The mourning and grief were terrible, but also there was so much remorse and guilt. I hadn't known that my son was ill and I would so much have liked to help him, to support him. And even if these guilt feelings had no basis, since I hadn't known anything about him, they kept coming back.

Whatever the circumstances of his disappearance, the loss of a child is beyond question the most inhuman trial it is possible to undergo. It's sheer misery. No one can imagine for themselves being deprived of all reason for living, even if this thought goes through the mind of every parent one day or another. To lose a child is to lose part of oneself. This atrocious sensation of being torn to pieces returns in the words of all the mothers to whom it has happened. The shock is so violent that sometimes even if the body is one great cry, the tears don't come.

So if I am with you today, it is in the hope perhaps of supporting as much as being supported, for to share a bit of my grief, but also hope and faith, is as important to me as it is to each one of you.'

'I entered the time of AIDS the day I learned that I was HIV positive. That's twenty years ago now. I don't want to shock anyone when I say that this news didn't come to me as a catastrophe. That was first of all because I had the irrational feeling that I would never fall ill, that I would be part of the ten per cent who, it was said at the time, would not perhaps die in the next three years.

I also had a plan, to risk the adventure of the religious life. The fact that I was HIV positive could not be a catastrophe. I had two excuses, the virus and chastity, for concealing under a bushel the sex drives which burdened me. In this realm it was no longer obligatory for me to engage in sex; quite the contrary. However incongruous it might seem, as a homosexual and Benedictine postulate my first reaction was: "You can never have a child." I was welcomed by the brothers of the community just as I was, it is just as I am that I live with my family and my friends, and it is just as I am that I have fallen in love and rediscovered the world that I never left.

I often have the feeling that the world which surrounds me, the people that I meet, aren't living in the time of AIDS but rather in the time after AIDS. It's a bit like "after the war". On 11 November, we commemorate the old soldiers of the First World War, whose survivors we can count on the fingers of one hand.

21

Unfortunately 1 December, the international day of action on AIDS and HIV, isn't a holiday, and as with 11 November there are fewer and fewer in the world to mobilize or remember, except that there has never been an armistice for AIDS. That's my fate: the death of my companion, the death of close friends. Today yet another has been taken into the care of a palliative aid agency. However, I too have the temptation to act as if I were living in the time after AIDS. I feel a little bit like a friend in a wheelchair who said to me one day, "Last night I dreamed that I was running." I would like to be able to dispense with condoms, I would like to forget the pill, but the medication is on the table. And this pill does not prevent me today from engaging in a loving and tender relationship, full of restraint, perhaps too much restraint.'

Part Two

Three Voices, Three Ways

Chapter 3

Sexuality, Democracy and Transcendence or, Who Fixes the Norms?

Eric Fassin

I begin with a topical issue – sexuality. Sexuality has a history: when we speak of it today we do so partly in the shadow of AIDS, which has led us to rethink sexual questions and their political significance. At the beginning of the 1980s it seemed as if we had come to the end of the politicization of sexual questions. During the 1970s we had seen all sorts of claims made by feminist and homosexual movements. These claims and the practices and arguments which supported them were formulated in terms of liberation. The 'laws of love' seemed to mark the end of sexual politics: the right to contraception and abortions, legislation on rape, the end of legal discrimination against homosexuals, in particular the age of consent. Sexuality seemed to have been liberated.

In the 1980s we saw the return of politicization in different terms. It was no longer simply a matter of tolerating the private life of homosexuals; it wasn't enough to say that everyone is free to do what he or she wants. In the time of AIDS, with the question of homosexuality, the argument went like this: when gays die of this illness, we must note that they are not just individuals but individuals involved in social relations. It is no longer enough to speak of individual practices, and not just because epidemiology invites us to think in terms of a statistical logic. By virtue of their consequences, sexual relations lead us to change our views: they involve individuals in society with a whole series of social bonds – with partners, family, friends, professionals, etc.

In short, here is a transition from individual practices to the recognition of social practices. What status does society accord to these people and thus to their relationships? This gives rise to debates on the homosexual couple (what are the rights of the surviving partner if one of them dies?), and beyond that on the homoparental family (what are the rights of homosexual parents?). In other words, the division between homosexuals, who are individual, on the one hand, and heterosexuals, whose status is guaranteed by the institutions of marriage and the family, on the other, being put in question. Thus the new politics is not practised so much around the recognition of a homosexual community as around a legitimating of homosexuality which puts the heterosexual norm in question.

In fact this political reformulation raises questions which affect norms and their status in our society. Formerly one could simply say: 'There are people, homosexuals, who do things which may seem to me to be regrettable, perhaps even detestable, but since I am modern and a liberal, I am going to tolerate them.' Now, by contrast, one says: 'There is no necessary reason for a society to institute a hierarchy in sexual matters, giving certain forms of behaviour, and not others, the legitimacy that the law brings and all the social organization that accompanies it.' So we have to investigate the norms that people want to legitimate in our society today. The sexual order is no longer so evident.

This is what is happening in connection with marriage. Hitherto it has been thought that marriage necessarily concerns two people of different sexes. If we take that view, aren't we saying that there is a hierarchy of sexual practices? While being tolerant, in this way aren't we presupposing that some (heterosexuals) are above others (homosexuals)? We haven't yet answered this question, but from all the evidence it is a disputed one. It didn't arise ten years ago but today it is open. The same goes for the definition of the family if one thinks of the claims for homoparentality: is the family so sacred that it has to be closed to homosexuals? And if that happens, hasn't a hierarchy of sexualities been set up?

This question of norms has been raised in a particularly acute way in connection with AIDS: there are all those ignored by the norm who would seem to be most directly the focus of the virus, whether these are homosexuals, prostitutes of both sexes or drug addicts. To keep to sexuality, it is no longer accepted that norms in this matter are self-evident. These norms are the object of discussions, of debates, of negotiations. In other words, there is no consensus (for or against opening up of marriage or filiation) and norms are no longer self-evident, in no need of explanation.

Consequently it is not only the content of the norms but also their status that has changed. Not only have new ideas, for example of freedom or equality, been introduced: our very relationship with the norms has been affected. On the one hand we must ask ourselves today whether we are always ready to say without hesitation that heterosexuality is better – and why. On the other hand, marriage, the family, sexual identity, sexuality, are no longer self-evident. And as they are open to question, the way in which norms are applied to us has been transformed. It is here, I believe, that the essential development is taking place today in the politicization of sexual questions: what is it that fundamentally defines norms – in their very principle?

TRANSCENDENCE AND SOCIETY

At this precise point sociological reflection meets up with religious reflection. Traditionally the norms are defined in a transcendent way, as being beyond or above society, over-hanging it or as its bedrock. There are supposed to be laws which don't need to be explained, since they assert themselves as being self-evident and not open to question. That is particularly true in the sexual order, where issues such as the subordinate place of women or the inferior status of homosexuality do not even need to be raised to be resolved. Where they have not simply been inherited by tradition, these laws, based on nature or revealed by God, by defin-ition escape historical change and political negotiation.

Norms functioning in this way do not necessarily have a religious reference. Science can play the same role, as we see in the debate on picture archiving and communication systems (PACS). In the name of transcendent scientific truths derived from anthropology or psychoanalysis, the immutable and indisputable, non-historical and non-political character of what is called the symbolic order has been defended. I am thinking of the invocations of Jacques Lacan or the imprecations of Pierre Legendre. It doesn't matter much whether the content is modern or traditional, it is the type of authority of the norm that defines the transcendence here. It is simply a matter of presupposing each time that the rules which organize society are not produced by society. They impose themselves a priori, independent of social agents.

This is precisely what is in process of shifting. The norms are increasingly defined in an immanent manner: by the interplay of social agents society itself defines not only its laws but also its norms. Neither the norm nor the law is posited as an a priori, indisputable fact. All at once yesterday's transcendent truths appear more as one set of discourses among others, subject like others to history and politics, to change and negotiation. The truths of knowledge today reveal themselves to be provisional truths; perhaps they will not be tomorrow's truths. That is true for psychoanalysis (we might think of the questioning of the Oedipus complex in this context); it is also true for anthropology (what becomes of the schemes of parenthood if it is no longer necessary to have an alternation of circles and triangles to mark the difference of the sexes in the alliance?). The status of truth is transformed here: in this immanent logic, truth, whether scientific or other, no longer appears definitive; on the contrary, it is provisional, indeed precarious.

I use the word transcendence in quite a broad way. It doesn't necessarily relate just to God but also to discourse which seeks to be resolutely secular, speaking in the name of science, but nevertheless has the same concern to be above society. Perhaps this rapprochement is less surprising than it might seem at first glance. During a debate on PACS, or rather arguing against PACS, Catholic bishops stated their position. The text that they published had no explicit religious reference. It did not use the words God, Jesus, gospel, and did not refer either to the Bible or to the church fathers. The argument was drawn from the human sciences. So we can well understand how there are different transcendences, in this case those of learned lay discourses and of religious discourses.

NORMS AND DEMOCRACY

So the question is that of the status of norms in a democratic society. What are they based on, if this is not the inherited authority of God, nature, tradition or even science? For me they no longer have an absolute foundation: they are the object of discussions, deliberations and negotiations. But it is not a matter of seeing here an end to norms and thus to the social bond which would swallow us up in a world of individuals with no cohesion. There has been a reversal of perspective: it is the debate on norms that today constitutes the social bond. In my view one can redefine laicity in this way, not so much in relation to laws but in relation to norms. Laicity does not so much affect the relationship between the state and religion as the relationship between norms and their foundations. Democratic laicity would then be the transition from a transcendent to an immanent definition of norms: in democracy these are not given once and for all, for eternity, but produced. They are not inherited but questioned, not imposed but negotiated. Democratic and lay societies are continually required to question their own rules. What was self-evident yesterday may perhaps become incomprehensible tomorrow.

To take a classical example, not related to sexual questions but to racial questions: originally the American Constitution, which presupposed free and equal citizens, nevertheless recognized slavery. This contradiction, written into the norms of American society, revealed itself in history – in particular at the time of the War of Independence. Here we see that to live democratically is not to fix the rules once and for all but to interrogate them as one goes along in the light of democratic principles which are discovered, i.e. the meaning of which one finds or which deepens on the way.

Inequality between men and women has been accepted in European societies: women did not have the right to vote in many countries until the Second World War. Today it seems self-evident that women must be able to vote. Perhaps the same thing will happen in the debates which preoccupy us today, on homosexual marriage and the homoparental family. What is at issue here in connection with democracy, which yesterday was unthinkable, could become self-evident tomorrow.

The symbolic order would then be revealed to be not a timeless order but a historical order, susceptible of evolution, open to deliberation. So democracy does not give rules once and for all; rather, it proposes a principle for questioning rules and norms.

We can understand why sexual questions have assumed such great significance in our societies today. After all, we could be amazed by it. While sexuality is certainly important, we don't spend our time having a sexuality. We do many other things. We might also find it amazing that the Catholic Church accords such importance to sexual questions and tell ourselves that there are other urgent matters in a world which seems to suffer from many other evils. Now even if I don't recognize myself in the perspective of the Vatican today – far from it – I believe that the church is right to attach considerable importance to these questions. For they are precisely the kind of questions which seem to be a sort of relic of transcendence.

We are well aware that the social order, the economic order, the natural order, are all historical and political. The taxes or the immigration which are debated in parliament are political. But we love to believe that this is not so in every case, that some things escape history and politics, things that are natural. We are tempted to think of sexual questions in the same terms. A man is a man and a woman is a woman. Of course they become couples. Now the self-evident nature of the difference between the sexes and heterosexuality is being put in question. In other words, I think that one can speak of an extension of the democratic domain to sexual questions.

The Vatican has understood this – even if so as to be disturbed about it. If we look at the *Lexicon On Ambiguous and Colloquial Terms About Family Life and Ethical Questions*, published in 2005 by the Pontifical Council for the Family, we find three articles on – or, we should rather say, against – the word 'gender'. Why so much passion? Because in effect to distinguish sex and genre, or nature and culture, is to think of the difference between the sexes as a social construct. If this 'constructionism' disturbs the church, it is because the sexual order has become susceptible to change, open to negotiation. It is no longer given once and for all, it is no longer the nature of things. The sexual order is the order of the sexes (hence the critiques of feminism and the 'collaboration between man and woman') and also the order of sexualities (hence the critiques of homosexual demands for the recognition of same-sex unions).

I emphasize that this redefinition of the symbolic order does not imply the end of norms. As the American philosopher Judith Butler asserts, I don't get up every morning, look at my wardrobe and ask myself whether I should dress as a man or a woman. We are not individuals free from every law, every rule, every norm: not everything is allowed, and one doesn't change sex as one changes shirts. For all that, the norms no longer impose themselves in an invisible way, without ever being questioned, as used to be the case. So there is some uncertainty. The conception of gender as a game (shall I put on trousers or a skirt, a tie or a ribbon?) seems to me to be less pertinent than a view – that of Judith Butler – in terms of 'trouble': there is trouble in the genre precisely because the norm is no longer given, because it proves to be a construct, and we have to live with this new relationship to norms.

So it is not a matter of a logic of individualization, but of the politicization of norms. That is true in the public sphere: the politicization of sexual questions can be seen in the numerous debates which agitate our societies, from homosexual marriage and homoparentality to violence towards women and sexual harassments, passing through prostitution, pornography, paedophilia, etc. It is also true in intimate personal life: one cannot, one can no longer, oppose the public sphere to private life, confining politics to the former and acting as if balances of power didn't exist in the latter. Both intimate life and the public arena are places where what is acceptable, what is to be wished and even what is desirable are played out. For example, this is what is being negotiated today between couples. Individual practices and representations are caught up in a political history, crossed by balances of power at the same time as by this history. They are inhabited by our public questions about freedom and equality. We are not simply determined by an eternal sexual nature; desire itself has a history and is a power issue. The relationship to norms is the place where sexual democracy is played out.

AN APPEAL

When I analyse the incompatibility of transcendence and democracy, or the idea that sexual democracy is based on immanence and not transcendence, it might be thought that this point of view is necessarily anti-religious. If there is no longer any place for transcendence in the definition of norms, what is left of religion? I believe that this is why the Vatican is disturbed and that for this reason it gives priority to the fight over sexual questions, with the feeling that if everything is open to history and politics, there is no longer transcendence in our societies and thus no longer religion. Nevertheless, today, this perspective has a cost for certain religious analyses, particularly since in order to find a transcendence the bishops base themselves not on revelation of tradition but on the human sciences. To provide a basis for a transcendence today they invoke the natural law.

The term 'natural' law has changed meaning since Thomas Aquinas. We hear it today as denoting the nature of things, their order as given. Nature is thus the tautology which says that a man is a man and a woman a woman. There seems to me to be a danger here which perhaps is not sufficiently perceived. If God is confused with nature, I am not sure that Christianity does very well here. On the contrary, hasn't one of the features of Christianity been precisely to reject this identification of God with nature? All that is, is not necessarily good. So it would seem costly to want to maintain transcendence in sexual questions by defining them by nature, which escapes history and politics. If my remarks might seem to put a religious perspective in question, I believe nevertheless that such criticisms are less dangerous from the point of view of Christianity than some forms of discourse which, in order to escape sexual democracy, tend to provide a basis for norms by confusing God with nature. My suggestion is rather an appeal to think in terms of a theology which is not naturalistic, and is democratic.

Chapter 4

To be Authentically Partners, the Energy of Differentiation

Lytta Basset

Sexuality as a human reality no longer seems to pose a problem today. It is largely thought to be natural and desirable; parents and families no longer interfere as they used to, moral and religious rules have very little impact. In consultations the talk is more of what hinders sexuality.

So it is important not to isolate sexuality. Sexuality is part of a whole which is the sexual relationship between two people who want to share each other in all their personal dimensions. We may note that in the lives of couples it is rarely sexuality as such which causes problems; rather, problems of relationship damage sexual life. So we have to work upwards. Doesn't harmony of bodies in a blossoming sexuality presuppose harmony of hearts and minds? Would a harmonious sexuality be possible in the long run without an authentic partnership at every level?

First of all one can argue that sex is what separates

us fundamentally. How can a man know what a woman experiences in the sexual act, to mention only the physical dimension? And confronted with the death of a child, how can a mother know precisely what the father feels? To be sexual is first of all to be differentiated, separate, indeed cut off from the other who – even while recognized as being the same – is primarily other, unknown, down to his or her body and intimacy.

The gospel invites all of us to a radical solitude: to stand all alone before God. Why? To explain our choices and actions. In the Bible God doesn't make a covenant with couples but with individuals, with persons responsible for themselves. 'You, follow me,' says Jesus, or 'Do you want to be healed?' The Protestant theologian Dietrich Bonhoeffer drew a distinction between the 'penultimate' things and the 'ultimate' things: whether I live a celibate life or as one of a couple, the primary thing is *my* relationship with God, and thus *my* eternal life. That is why what I say is to be seen in relative terms; however, this is a relativity which touches on essentials.

THE BREAK

The process of life is violent and painful: it begins with birth. It's the same with life according to the Spirit – this birth in the wind and from the wind of which Jesus speaks in John 3. One can say that the gospel shakes, addresses, doesn't beat about the bush: 'Do not suppose that I have come to bring peace to the earth,' warned Jesus. 'It is not peace that I have come to bring but the sword. For I have come to set son against father, daughter against mother,

38

daughter-in-law against mother-in law; a person's ene-
mies will be members of his own household' (Matthew
10.34–36).

So this is a break between those who most resemble
each other: son–father, daughter–mother, etc. It is a
differentiation which implies a more or less painful
process, in adolescence or much later. And it is a
differentiation which is initiated by God himself, since
there is no question of wielding the sword oneself, in a
voluntaristic way: it is more a matter of consenting to
the process. Why doesn't Christ's sword also go explicitly
between the spouses? Beyond question because it is
important for it to begin by differentiating each spouse
from the preceding generation.

Now the image of the sword already appears in Genesis
3.24, when the mythical couple of Adam and Eve leave the
garden of Eden: then 'in front of the Garden of Eden God
posted the great winged creatures and the fiery flashing
sword, to guard the way to the tree of life'. There is no
precise parallel to this 'fiery flashing sword, to guard the
way to the tree of life'. One might think of the Pentecost
story, in which 'there appeared to them tongues as of fire;
these separated and came to rest on the head of each one
of them' (Acts 2.3). It is as if the fire of differentiation,
under the symbolic form of the sword, did not cease to
'flash', guarding for ever the way to the tree of life which is
accessible to human beings differentiated from one another.
This is a tree of life which one could call 'tree of the living',
since the word is in the plural in Hebrew, a life where there
is room for everyone because the differentiation provides
shelter from violence and exclusion.

We can likewise note the radical character of the gospel in Luke 14.26, which recommends that one should hate the relatives with whom one has fused: 'Anyone who comes to me without hating father, mother, wife, children, brothers, sisters, yes even his own life,' says Jesus, 'cannot be my disciple' – it doesn't happen. We mustn't tone down and minimize such 'hatred' as numerous translations tend to do; it goes with this indispensable break, including that between spouses. Here we touch on a great anthropological truth: haven't the psychological sciences taught us that there is no authentic love – and therefore no healthy and harmonious sexuality – which does not become aware of the aggression and the hatred that differentiate human beings from those close to them and allow them to become fully subjects?

From the book of Genesis onwards the Bible uses extremely realistic language: 'This is why the man *abandons* his father and mother and attaches himself to his wife' (2.24). Isn't that stronger than the 'leaves' which is adopted by numerous translations? It isn't a matter of simply moving out but of a radical break which, far from being natural and spontaneous, can appear very unpopular. But without such a process one continues to idealize one's parents, and links this with the fantasy of the ideal spouse. Countless couples destroy themselves, and their sexuality, because the partners have not been differentiated from their respective parents. Granted, this is difficult: it invites one to accept being 'abandoned' by the near one who differentiates himself or herself and to 'abandon' him or her to their own destiny. But it is possible to abandon this other to something greater than oneself, to abandon them in the sense of trusting in God. And in a homosexual relationship this is all the more important, since the risk of fusion is greater.

LACK

To talk of desire is to talk of lack, of not being self-sufficient. Now if I use someone else to fill my lack, certainly the lack disappears, but so does my desire. The relationship is constantly put in danger by the unconscious quest for the mother's womb – by the need to fuse. The Bible suggests that the lack must remain because it is an integral part of the human condition. 'The Lord God made the *adam* fall into a deep sleep', relates Genesis. 'And while he was asleep God took one of his ribs and closed the flesh up again forthwith' (2.21). In the twelfth century the famous Jewish commentator Rashi translated the Hebrew word as 'the side'. Doesn't that express the painful experience of lack? 'I am lacking one side', in other words, 'I have no one beside me.' I am asked to accept the lack and the absence – in order to appreciate the presence of another at my side. In his *Nicomachean Ethics* (Book IX 9, 1169b), Aristotle said that the friend provides what one is incapable of providing for oneself. The trap, which is also there for couples, is to have someone at one's side while hiding the fact that one still has a lack in oneself.

In this perspective we can see the degree to which sexuality can find as a parasite on it the fear of being abandoned and confronted with one's empty interior. So the constant need to be reassured involves devouring sexual relations. And the circle becomes a vicious one: fear, anxiety, possessiveness, love–fusion–confusion, the failure of the attempt to fill the void, fear, anxiety, etc. Neither of the partners allows the other to be himself or herself, in other words to confront his or her own wounds, the excruciating sequels to his or her own past. Neither sees that they are advised to 'abandon' the other to God, in other words to the one who can little by little lead them to who they are in truth. So it is that in giving deadly fruit to her partner to eat, Eve thinks that she is filling him. In fact she is supplying his lack by eliminating the other. The features of union present in the Hebrew text say a lot about the fusion–confusion–lack of differentiation of the couple: 'She also gave some to her husband who was with her, and he ate it' (Genesis 3.6).

RENUNCIATIONS

It is impossible to become authentically partners without accepting some major renunciations:

The renunciation of the imaginary other: to want him or her to be what they are not, for example by her constantly feeding his sexual fantasies, or by him being sentimental to order. And conversely, to refuse to correspond completely to the other's expectations.

The renunciation of projections: the renunciation of projecting on to one's spouse that part of oneself which one rejects, first of all by becoming aware of it. The classic example is guilt: it is the unfaithful husband who, on returning home unable to bear his guilt feelings, gets rid of them by blaming his wife even more. Another example: someone may reproach the other for his or her lack of courage, failing to recognize their own fear. On every occasion it is fruitful to ask oneself: couldn't it be that when I'm criticizing my partner, I'm talking about myself? The psychoanalyst Guy Corneau writes: 'The couple can become the place of intense work upon oneself from the moment one accepts the notion that everything which irritates us in the other could be an unknown part of ourselves.'[1]

The renunciation of devouring or fusing: to accept that my great love doesn't understand me and perhaps has a diametrically opposed opinion, doesn't share all my convictions, my faith, what is essential for me. To accept the impression sometimes of having sexual relations with a stranger. But also to learn to see all this as an occasion for growing in the unconditional acceptance of the other. Making an effort to look at as Jesus looked at the rich man of the gospel: 'He looked at him and loved him' (Mark 10.21), because he loved his money so much that he wasn't (yet) ready to change!

The renunciation of absolute knowledge: 'of Good and Evil, the good and the bad', a definitive knowledge which belongs only to God.[2] One has to leave to the other his or her part in the mystery and beyond that, the mystery of his or her origin; one has to renounce saying, even after decades of life together, 'I know him or her as if I had made them.' Isn't that what the symbolism of the Genesis text suggests: 'The Lord God made the *adam* fall into a deep sleep' (2.21)? That amounts to saying that the terrestrial creature (which does not yet have a sex) will never know the origin of the other (of whom it is made), any more than it will know its future, for it does not know what this other bears within itself; it was asleep when the other was being made and its knowledge of the other is too partial for it to be able to assert 'You will never change.'

The renunciation of domination: unless they have accepted these renunciations, the couple will only see the arduous aspect of life ('spines and thorns', 'pain' and 'sweat of the brow'). The couple is reduced to relations of domination and thus of violence. It is God who identifies the root of the problem when addressing the woman: 'He will dominate you.' That is the fruit of fusion: she will be attached to the man as an identical part of him, and he will speak to God exclusively in the first person as if she did not exist. And to dominate is to annihilate: one exists only as other. On the other hand, when one is differentiated neither is more nor less, but each is simply different, irreducible in his or her difference, and so can no longer be 'dominated'. The renunciation of domination is to let loose of the other and centre oneself on who one is, to reach the hard core of one's identity which proves indestructible. No violence, even sexual violence, will finish off this 'me'.

How does one make progress in renunciation? By dialogue, in the course of which I discover that the problem is (also) in me: that it comes from wounds, dysfunctions, confusions linked to my past. I adopt the course of accepting this vulnerable part and dealing with it, rather than continuing systematically to make my partner responsible. Now it may be that this accepted vulnerability ends up by affecting the partner who believes himself or herself invincible – and by bringing him or her closer. As Paul Ricoeur writes: 'A self mindful of the vulnerability of the mortal condition can accept the weakness of a friend better if it does not draw on its own reserves of strength.'[3] Behind the dysfunctioning projected on my spouse I begin to perceive the presence of the Christ, which draws me out of the fortress in which I was 'always right'.

THE BOND OF PARTNERSHIP

'I don't have three children, but four,' say some mothers. The partnership is often put in peril by the impossibility of being able to count on the spouse. But here, too, there is a vicious circle: the less I accept the other, the more I do in his or her place, the more I take upon myself . . . and the more he or she is demotivated. One can advance only if one does not take the place of the other, i.e. fuse. And that brings us back to the sword: only a break allows an authentic partnership.[4] In the Genesis story there is break and differentiation, with the symbolism of the 'extraction' from the side. But what motivates this action is taking human solitude into account and the divine desire to establish a fruitful partnership: 'I shall make him a helper' (2.18). The Hebrew term is neuter, '*ezer*', and not the feminine '*ezrah*', which one would expect. So this moment in the narrative is about every type of relationship between human beings and not exclusively about the man–woman relationship: this can be a partnership between two men or two women, without sexuality ever being involved.

Now this term *'ezer'* is for the most part used of God in the Hebrew Bible – and in situations of extreme distress, when a human being has no issue and God becomes his 'helper'. Here we are in the first book of the Bible and, even before God, the other human being is presented as a real 'helper'. Before the question of amorous and sexual relations even arises, another is presented as the 'helper of a terrestrial creature who has been given over to a "solitude" which is "not good"' (Genesis 2.18). So according to the Bible the sexual partner is first of all a neighbour. Thus God says, 'I will make for him a helper corresponding to him'. We find nothing feminine in this expression. The construction is unique in the Bible. It is as if at the basic structure of the human being there is an 'I' who is partner of a 'you'. 'Corresponding' suggests 'response', 'responsible': we could say that the otherness is posited before the sexual difference, even before the 'woman' is created (v. 23) and there is any question of procreation (v. 24). Emmanuel Levinas emphasizes that the other is created to evoke my response, to show me my responsibility: 'Responsibility for this other – closer than any proximity and yet unknown.'[5]

By contrast, the man of Genesis 3 shows himself to be irresponsible when he attributes the failure of the inter-human relationship to God. 'It was the woman you put with me; she gave me some fruit from the tree, and I ate it' (3.12). Rather, the question must be asked:

'What response did I give to Eve?' Thus in many couples who function more or less in a sado-masochistic way the 'response' given to the sadist is sheer passiveness and irresponsibility. An authentic partnership presupposes the constant fidelity of each to himself or herself. This is a fidelity that is certainly more fundamental than fidelity to the other, which so often hides a terrible alienation. In a harmonious partnership two fidelities respond to each other and adjust. As Gabriel Marcel writes, 'In a sense I can only be faithful to my own commitment, that is, it seems, to myself.'[6]

INTIMACY BECOMES POSSIBLE AGAIN

If the partnership is the bond in the differentiation, we can see the likeness in the intimacy. For the man in the Genesis account, this is becoming aware of what he has in common with the woman – and that makes him speak for the first time: 'This one at last is bone of my bone and flesh of my flesh . . .' (Genesis 2.23). As Paul Ricoeur says, 'The similitude (of 'as yourself') is the fruit of the exchange between self-esteem and solicitude for the other'.[7]

Sexuality then proves harmonious in the relationship: I have arrived at what is human in me; I have integrated the history of my wounds and what has followed them; I have rediscovered self-esteem. And I greet what is profoundly human in the other. So I no longer fear the one who comes (too) close to me, I no longer fear proximity. Guy Corneau calls that 'the love of friendship', a love which cannot be reduced to the sexual relationship. 'How many couples can truly say that they love each other in a friendly way?', he asks. Often the fusion is such that 'we cannot hear from our partner a quarter of what a friend could tell us . . . However, one of the factors which contributes most to the creation of true intimacy is friendship . . . Friendship allows the couple to breathe, it represents a more solid and more durable basis than sexuality for establishing a long-term relationship.'[8] In fact, friendship is based on an authentic communication which is grounded in a word that expresses feeling without judging.

Beyond question this was the nature of Jesus' relations with his disciples, Mary Magdalene in particular. At this level of communication, physical union is no longer necessary. What matters in Christian life, then, is to succeed in keeping oneself *monos*, alone, before God. In this sense there is a monastic vocation for everyone, even in the life of a couple. One is invited to give God first place in one's life, without this being to the detriment of one's spouse. Finally, we should remember that the only biblical book which is about the relationship of the couple (including their sensual and sexual relationship), the Song of Songs, speaks in an exclusively poetic way, as if to encourage us always to allow the relationship its dimension of mystery, its divine dimension.

NOTES

1. Guy Corneau, *N'y a-t-il pas d'amour heureux?*, R. Laffont 1997, p. 39.
2. Cf. my interpretation of Genesis 2–3 in *Guérir du malheur*,

Albin Michel 1999. Since the 'tree of the knowledge of good and evil' and the 'tree of life' are in the same place, 'in the middle of the garden', one can think that to lay one's hand on another, claiming to know him or her perfectly, amounts to laying one's hand on the Living One.

3. Paul Ricoeur, *Soi-même comme un autre*, Seuil 1990, p. 224.
4. Cf. the covenant rite in the Hebrew Bible: someone who wanted to engage in a solid and durable covenant would cut an animal in two, as if it was necessary first to differentiate clearly in a symbolic way the two parties who were making the covenant.
5. Emmanuel Levinas, *Du sacré au saint. Cinq nouvelles lectures talmudiques*, Éditions de Minuit 1977, ch. 4: 'Et Dieu créa la femme', p. 133. The Reformer Jean Calvin and the exegete Claus Westermann both noted this priority given to otherness in the earliest creation account.
6. Gabriel Marcel, *Être et avoir*, Aubier 1935, p. 56.
7. Ricoeur, *Soi-même comme un autre* (n. 3), p. 226.
8. Corneau, *N'y a-t-il pas d'amour heureux?* (n. 1), pp. 259f.

Chapter 5

This is My Body, Given for You: Christianity and Sexuality

Timothy Radcliffe

I have been asked to think with you about Christianity and sexuality. I do so with some hesitation. First of all as a celibate priest, I cannot claim to have practical experience on which to base my reflections. When priests talk about sex, then we easily become ridiculous.

Our society is obsessed by sex, even in England, despite comments of a previous French prime minister about the virility of English men! But our culture lacks a profound reflection upon what it means for us to be sexual beings. Christianity ought to offer a deep vision of sexuality, but the media usually present the church's interest in sexuality in terms of control. The church is seen as deciding what is permitted and what is forbidden. It is true that every human society, throughout history, has had rules about sexual behaviour, but we have need of more than rules if we are to understand our sexuality. When I was in Rome, I tried to explain to my brethren why cricket is the most beautiful game in the world. Telling them the rules of cricket would not be enough to show the point of playing cricket. One does not play cricket in order to obey the rules, even if the rules are necessary.

The church does have a reflection on sexuality that is based on the natural law. This is illuminating, but often it has given us a very limited appreciation of sexuality which focuses mainly on the begetting of children. Sexual intercourse is often seen narrowly in terms of reproduction. So I would like to start elsewhere, with the event that is at the heart of Christianity, the Last Supper. On that night Jesus gathered the disciples around him, and he took bread, blessed it and gave it to them saying, 'This is my body, given for you.'

At the heart of our religion is the gift of a body. I believe that one can best get a glimpse of the depth and beauty of sexuality by looking at the Last Supper. It teaches us what it means to give our bodies to other people. Sexuality also helps us to understand the Last Supper. So I will argue that we can best understand sexuality in the light of the Eucharist, and the Eucharist in the light of our sexuality. I argued this recently in a book called *What is the Point of being a Christian?*[1] In the book I focused mainly on our affectivity. I looked at how sexual desire can be deformed by fantasy that may lead us into infatuation or lust. I argued that we need to come down to earth and learn to desire well, as the human beings that we are, with the histories and commitments that we have. Here I wish to do something a bit different. I will focus more directly on sexuality. What can the Last Supper teach us about how to live our sexuality well, and with beauty? How can our sexuality really be Eucharistic?

THIS IS MY BODY

We start with the words 'This is my body.' What does it mean to be bodily? For much of the history of the West there has been a sharp dichotomy between the body and the spirit, the soul or the mind. We have tended to despise the body as a rather unworthy receptacle for what really matters, the non-physical part of us. And especially since the seventeenth century we have been seduced by the idea that it is our minds that really matter. *Cogito ergo sum.* And this means that communication and human community is usually seen in terms of the mind. I communicate with you by sending messages from my mind to your minds. Here I am with thoughts about sexuality in my mind, and I am trying to get past all the obstacles of our bodies, so that you may receive the messages in your minds. It is as if I am like the captain of a ship sending radio messages, and hoping that someone out there is picking up the messages and deciphering them.

If you think like that, and most people do, then bodies are not important. They are even an obstacle to communication. If only we could be pure minds, then we would be in immediate communion with each other, without the possibility of misunderstanding.

Jesus' words at the Last Supper take us back to an older tradition. The human body is the basis of all communication. It is because we are bodily that we can be in touch with each other. We can see, hear, smell and touch each other. It is as if our bodies were tools of communication, like a telephone, to get messages

53

from one mind to another. The human body is of itself deeply communicative. Through our bodies we are present to each other. When human beings became capable of language, if we could have been called human prior to that even, then we did not leave our bodily communication behind, as if it was second class. Being able to talk gave our bodily communication a deeper meaning, a new depth.

Let us start with food. Every living being must eat. Bacteria eat, but I doubt whether they find it very exciting. They have no *nouvelle cuisine!* I do not imagine that they discuss the menu with pleasure. They just eat so as to survive. But when we think of animals, then we can see that eating acquires a new significance, a deeper meaning. For most animals, eating is not just a physical necessity, it is part of being in community, sharing a common world.

Think of lions. When a pride of lions eats a zebra, the meal binds the pride together, and expresses its nature. The old male lion, I think, eats first, and then the lionesses get their turn, and finally the lion cubs have a chance to finish off whatever is left. This fundamental physical activity shows what it means to be a member of that community of lions.

When human beings eat together, then eating should acquire an even deeper meaning, if we resist the temptation of fast food. It is not just that we talk while we are eating, but the fact that we are talking animals means that our eating expresses a deeper communion. We eat to celebrate friendship, to sustain families, to make contact with business partners, to celebrate birthdays. We feast and fast. We eat to remember the past and to hope for the future. And so it was that when Jesus wished to establish the new covenant between God and humanity, he gathered the disciples for a meal. He blessed and broke the bread and shared it. Eating did not just become the ingestion of nutrition, but expressed the common life of divinity and humanity.

And so it is with that other fundamental animal activity, which is sexual intercourse. Bacteria reproduce, but I do not expect that it is very exciting. Lions have sex, and this too is an expression of communion. Which lions have sex with which lionesses says a lot about each lion's place in the pride. When a young lion succeeds in having intercourse with a senior lioness, then the old lion that rules the pride knows that his days are numbered. Soon he will be expelled.

Because we humans are linguistic beings, then sexual intercourse is given an even deeper meaning. It becomes a fundamental expression of how we are in communion with one another. It is not that we speak before or after having sex, though that matters. It is that sexual behaviour should be communicative. It should be expressive of who are the people involved. It is a way of speaking deeply.

Let's take the kiss. In Ireland fifty years ago, it was notorious that the clergy used to try to regulate kisses. People were told how long they could kiss, maybe ten seconds if you were under eighteen! And there were rules about what sorts of kisses were allowed. The most dangerous kiss of all was known as the French kiss. But it is better to reflect upon what a kiss says. The body is made to be communicative, and the face is the apex of the body's communication. The face shows what it means to be bodily, and the mouth, speaking and kissing, expresses the culmination of communication.

This brings me to the most important point that I wish to make. When we think of Christianity and sexuality, then people usually ask what is permitted or forbidden. What sexual activity is permitted between people who are not married? Can people of the same sex have a sexual relation? But this is to start at the wrong place. The first question in all ethics is: 'What does my behaviour say?' To quote Herbert McCabe OP, 'Ethics is just the study of human behaviour in so far as it is a piece of communication, in so far as it says something or fails to say something.'[2] Ethics is learning to behave to each other so that we relate ever more deeply. An action is not bad because it is forbidden but because it undermines human communion, though if it obviously does do that, then it may be good to forbid it.

So it is natural that when Jesus wishes to express the utter communion of God and humanity, then he does so by giving his body. He is not giving us a lump of matter. He is making a sign that speaks and creates communion.

GIVEN FOR YOU

And Jesus says that this body is given for you. It is gift. As I explain at some length in *What is the Point of Being a Christian?*, this can be hard for our society to understand. What does it means for Jesus to give us his body? This may be incomprehensible because for the last four hundred years we have tended to think of bodies as possessions. Human dignity is founded on the ownership of possession. In the Underground in London I came across an advertisement for a book on the human body called, if I remember correctly, *Man: from 12000 BC until today. All models, shapes, sizes and colours. Haynes Owners Workshop Manual.* It was the sort of owner's manual that one receives with a car or a washing machine.

If one thinks that one's body is fundamentally an important possession among others, then of course one can do what one likes with it, as long as it harms no one else. I can do what I like with my car. I can sleep in it, or use it to race, or just let it rot or grow flowers in it. It is mine to dispose of as I wish. The result has been a sexual ethic which has often been founded on the rights of possession. Usually a man was seen as owning not only his own body but also the body of his wife. He could do what he liked with her, though she did not possess his body in the same way. Adultery by the woman was seen as a form of robbery, since in sleeping with another man she would be unlawfully disposing of her husband's property. It was usually more acceptable for a man to do what he wished with his own body, since he owned it.

When Jeremy Bentham, a famous nineteenth-century English social thinker, died, he left his body to University College, London. It is stuffed and you can see it in the main hall. When there is a meeting of the governing body of the college, then the body is brought in. But Jesus was doing something far more profound by his act. When he gave us his body, he was expressing the deepest meaning of what it is to be a body. To be a body is to receive all that is from one's parents and their parents before them. It is ultimately to receive one's being from God. Our existence is a gift in every moment. God gives me being now.

So our sexual relations should be expressive of the gift of oneself to another, and the acceptance of the gift which is the being of the other person. When I kissed my mother good night, this was expressive of my reverence for the one who gave me life. And our sexual relationships should be deeply expressive of gift. I learn how to give myself to another without reserve, with trust and confidence. I learn how to receive the gift that is the other person with reverence and gratitude. A married couple could sleep together, and yet not give themselves to each other or fail to receive the gift of the other person's body.

So these words of the Last Supper take us to the heart of a sexual ethic. Sexuality is about communion; it speaks. And what it should express is mutual generosity, the giving and the receiving of gifts. But the Last Supper was also the moment at which Jesus faced and embraced the contradiction of communion. On that night he shared himself with Judas who had sold him, with Peter who would shortly deny him, and with the other disciples who would mostly run away. It was the dark night, when there was betrayal, lies, fear, violence and death. On that night Jesus faced all that subverts and destroys human communion. He faced and transcended it.

This means that a Christian sexual ethic should be more than just a nice ideal which we try to follow as best we can. If it is based on the Last Supper, then it should help us to face failure in our mutual relationships and transcend it. The Eucharist is the sacrament of hope, because on that night, when there was apparently nothing to hope for, Jesus performed this astonishing gift of himself. And a Christian sexual ethic should help us to live with hope, in the face of our own failures and denials and betrayals of each other.

Let's look at how Jesus faced the dramas of that night and transcended them. He was faced with lies, domination, betrayal and death. A good sexual ethic should help us to do that.

LIES

Human sexuality is, we have seen, about the building of communion. It speaks. It creates communion. But at the Last Supper, we see the collapse of language. Communication breaks down. Judas betrays Jesus. He performs the profoundly untruthful act of treating Jesus as if he were not a human being but a piece of merchandise, to be sold for thirty pieces of silver. Peter says that he will lay down his life for Jesus, but when the moment comes he lies. Three times he denies that he knows Jesus: 'Woman, I do not know him' (Luke 22.57). In face of all this violence and untruth, Jesus becomes silent. He has nothing to say. As the prophet Isaiah wrote, 'He was oppressed and afflicted, and yet he opened not his mouth; like a lamb that is led to the slaughter and like that before its shearers is dumb, so he opened not his mouth' (Isaiah 53.7).

The death of Jesus looks like the defeat of language. The Word of God is silenced. And yet the Word rises from the dead and appears to the disciples and says,

'Peace be with you.' He turns to Peter and heals his threefold denial. Three times, in John's Gospel, he asks Peter whether he loves him, and so overcomes the three lies that Peter had told.

Bad sexual behaviour usually involves lies. When David sleeps with Bathsheba, the wife of Uriah the Hittite, then his sin is not just that he has performed a forbidden sexual act. He is caught up in lies and violence. When Uriah comes home, David tries to deceive him. He wishes to get Uriah drunk so that he will go and sleep with his wife and then think that the child is his own. This doesn't work. Finally he writes to the commander of his army that Uriah must be sent out into the most dangerous fighting, so that he will be killed.

A Christian sexual ethic teaches us to speak truthfully with our bodies, and to overcome the lies that we may sometimes tell. When you have sexual intercourse with someone, you say with your body, 'I give myself to you, without reserve, now and for ever, and I receive all you are as a gift.' But if we get up early the next morning and leave a note by the bed saying, 'Thanks for the pleasurable sex, but I never wish to see you again,' we have, in a sense, lied with our bodies. It is as if we were to say, 'I love you eternally' and then walk away for ever. We need to touch each other truthfully, to mean what we say when we kiss. We need to live out the deep meaning of what we do with each other's bodies.

But if a Christian sexual ethic is to be hopeful, then it must teach us how to say the words that heal the wounds when we lie. We need to find the words that break the silence and restore communion. It is not enough just to go to confession and get absolution. We need to give and receive absolution from each other. To live out our sexuality truthfully means also that we find ways to overcome the lies and heal the hurts.

DOMINATION

The Last Supper was also a moment in which communion broke down because of violence and domination. Jesus was the victim of force. He was bought by the rich and the powerful. He was taken away by the force of soldiers, and nailed to a tree. But Jesus replied at the Last Supper to all this violence with pure vulnerability. He placed himself in the hands of the disciples, knowing what they would do. He refused to protect himself. Even though they would deny him, he would not deny them.

Bad sexual behaviour is usually linked with domination and violence. We can see this again with David and Bathsheba. It is the strong and powerful king who takes the wife of the soldier and then organizes his death. All over the world today, one can see the violence that often accompanies sex. War is always associated with the rape of women, but women are daily forced to submit to the domination of men, who force them to have sex. Once again we can see how the question of what is permitted or forbidden does not get to the heart of a sexual ethic. As John Paul II said, a man may rape even his own wife. Think of the millions of children who are forced into sex with foreign tourists in Thailand and the Philippines. Whenever dominance is introduced into a sexual relationship, the heart of our sexuality is denied.

The Last Supper teaches us that the heart of a Christian sexual ethic is the renunciation of violence. We seek mutuality and equality. When someone desires the body of another person, that desire should not be rapacious, seeking to take possession of the body, as if it were a piece of meat to be devoured. We must learn to desire in a way that delights in the other, that treasures his or her vulnerability, that takes pleasure in his or her very existence. We must delight in another as God delights in us, tenderly and without dominion. In so far as there is a taking possession, it is to be mutual. As St Paul said, 'For the wife does not rule over her own body but the husband does; likewise the husband does not rule over his own body, but the wife does' (1 Corinthians 7.4).

Desire too finds its depth in mutuality. We desire to be desired, and treasure the other's desire for us. We take pleasure in another taking pleasure in ourselves. We take the immense risk of letting ourselves be seen by the other, in all our vulnerability, of placing ourselves in their hands. Rowan Williams, the Archbishop of Canterbury and a married man, has written about this beautifully:

All this means, crucially, that in sexual relation I am no longer in charge of what I am. Any genuine experience of desire leaves me in something like this position: I cannot of myself satisfy my wants without distorting or trivializing them. But here we have a particularly intense case of the helplessness of the ego alone. For my body to be the cause of joy, the end of homecoming, for me, it must be there for someone else, be perceived, accepted, nurtured; and that means being given over to the creation of joy in that other, because only as directed to the enjoyment, the happiness, of the other does it become unreservedly lovable. To desire my joy is to desire the joy of the one I desire: my search for enjoyment through the bodily presence of another is a longing to be enjoyed in my body... We are pleased because we are pleasing.[3]

So the Last Supper invites us to share the immense vulnerability of Jesus, as he places himself in the hands of the disciples. It is the vulnerability that he bears for ever. When he rises from the dead, he shows the disciples his wounds in his hands and his side. He is for ever the wounded and risen Christ.

Do we dare to learn such vulnerability to another? Do we dare to take the risk of being wounded by the one whom we love? Belief in the resurrection means that we trust that the wounds we receive are not unto death and so we dare to take the risk of getting hurt.

If a good sexual relationship overcomes the distortions of power, reaching for equality and mutuality, then it is a preaching of the gospel to the society in which we live. It challenges the unjust power structures of every society. All too often relationships merely echo the patterns of dominance of the society. If society is ruled by men, then men will probably rule in the home and in the bed. So a good sexual ethic offers a challenge that is implicitly political. If we are formed in our homes for reciprocity, then we will not be at home in political structures that oppress.

BETRAYAL

The Last Supper was a moment of supreme hurt to a relationship, betrayal. Judas hands his friend over to death. This is the ultimate rejection of communion. And yet Jesus is not a simple victim. He transforms the betrayal into a gift. This is a supremely creative act. He is handed over to the authorities to be killed. But at the Last Supper he grasps this and makes it a handing over for the new covenant. He is given over to death, but he makes it a promise of life and forgiveness. And in his last words to Judas, he still addresses him as a friend: 'Friend, why are you here?' He waits for Peter on the other side of death with forgiveness. He is faithful. So every Eucharist is a celebration of creative fidelity.

So at the heart of a Christian sexual ethic is fidelity. We give ourselves, our bodies, our lives, our hopes and fears, to another unreservedly, now and for ever. The typical form that this has taken throughout Christian history has been through the marriage vows, when a husband and a wife pledge mutual fidelity until death. This has become much more difficult in our society, in which people live much longer, and are more mobile. Marriage is a fragile institution. In fact in our society no bonds are as secure as they used to be. We live in a society of short-term contracts, whether at work or at home. And this creates immense problems for couples whose marriages have broken down and who find themselves in 'irregular situations'.

However, the purpose of this discussion is not to focus on the rules and consider whether people should be allowed to remarry after divorce. I wish to get back to the fundamental principles. And at the heart of sexual ethics, I argue, must be the cherishing of fidelity, whatever the form of relationship we have. Even in friendship fidelity is essential.

Fidelity is much deeper than simply not getting divorced. It is offering a context in which people take the time to belong to another, to see the other and be seen. It takes time to dare enter into intimacy and vulnerability. It takes time to learn how to be free and transparent in the presence of another. The longer that I am with another, the more he or she will discover my weakness, my fears and failings. Fidelity is risky. Once again, Rowan Williams says it beautifully:

> I can only fully discover the body's grace in *taking time,* the time needed for a mutual recognition that my partner and I are not simply passive instruments to each other. Such things are learned in the fabric of a whole relation of converse and co-operation; yet of course the more time taken, the longer a kind of risk endures. There is more to expose, and a *sustaining* of the will to let oneself be formed by the perceptions of another. Properly understood, sexual faithfulness is not an avoidance of risk, but the creation of a context in which grace can abound because there is a commitment not to run away from the perception of another.[4]

One needs courage to remain with another when he or she begins to see one's weakness. The Eucharist invites us to endure in fidelity, when we are exposed in all our fragility.

DEATH

At the Last Supper Jesus and the disciples face death. Death is the ultimate enemy of human communion, the final breakdown of communication. Death silences the words that we speak to each other and even to God. As the psalm says, 'The dead do not praise the Lord, nor do those who go down into silence' (Psalm 115.17). But in the face of death, Jesus offers us his body. This is the sacrament of a community in which death is embraced and transcended. It is the community of the living and the dead, the communion of saints.

Faced with death, we often have little to say, but Jesus has given us something to do. We do what he did, taking bread, blessing it and sharing it. I remember a terrible day in Rwanda, of which I have often spoken. It was a day upon which violence was breaking out in the whole country. We travelled north, negotiating our way through barricades of soldiers and rebels. We were stopped by groups of masked men with machetes and swords. We then visited refugee camps, with thousands of people living under plastic sheets; we went to a hospital filled with children who had lost their limbs. That night, with the sisters, I found that I was lost for words. In the face of so much suffering, what could one say? But we had something to do, what Jesus had done, in memory of him.

When we offer our body to another person, saying 'This is my body, given to you', then what does that say in the face of death? Does a Christian sexual ethic offer hope in the face of death, our own and that of those whom we love?

There is a deep link between sex and death. In the Old Testament, the begetting of children was the principal hope of immortality. One goes down to the silence of the grave, but one's children would speak one's name. One would be immortal in the memory of one's offspring. So sexuality was our defiance of death. That is why one had a duty to raise up children for one's brother if he were to die without issue. But Jesus argues with the Sadducees that the resurrection makes this no longer necessary. If we are raised from the dead, then we do not need the vicarious immortality of children. So the resurrection transforms the relationship between sexuality and death. Sexual intercourse is no longer our only chance of survival beyond the grave. Sex does not defy death just by providing us with children.

Sex and death are still linked today. For most of Christian history, the bearing of children was a time of extreme danger for women. The giving of life went with the risk of death. And now in our days, there is the link with AIDS, especially for women in poor countries, where they have no control over when and with whom they have sex. In Africa, for example, sex can so often be fatal.

So what can a Christian sexuality offer us in the face of death? It is not just the delegated immortality of children, though that does indeed reveal the profound creativity of human sexuality in the face of mortality. Also we give our bodies to each other as an act of love which is stronger than death. The Song of Songs says, 'Set me as a seal upon your heart, as a seal upon your arm, for love is as strong as death' (8.6). But in Christ, love is stronger than death. The love of the Father for the Son triumphs over death. If our sex really is, as we say, 'an act of love', then death cannot defeat it. Sexual relations should express that love of the Father for the Son which defeats our old enemy.

CONCLUSION

Our society is obsessed with sex, yet lacks a deep exploration of its meaning. Christianity ought to offer a vision of the beauty and significance of human sexuality. Often our witness is stifled because all that the church teaches is heard in terms of laws, what is forbidden or permitted. The church is seen as a sexual policeman. Of course rules are necessary and useful, but they have to express a shared understanding of what it means to be sexual in the first place. When the church does articulate a vision of sexuality it is usually in terms of the natural law. This has its own usefulness and beauty, and I do not wish to dismiss it at all, but it carries the danger the sex may then be seen reductively, in terms of the production of children. Sexuality must be placed again in the complex context of human communication, with defeats and victories.

On the night before he died, Jesus gave us his body, and this invites us to a deeper understanding of what it might mean to offer our body to another person. It is an act of communication. It should speak, therefore, of who we are and for what we long. Sexuality should be communicative. Above all it speaks a relationship that is founded in the giving and receiving of gifts. At the heart of sexuality is gratitude and generosity. Sexual intercourse is the transmission of the gift of our being, and so a profound expression of what it means to be human.

Jesus did not just enact a sign of communion. He did what he did in the face of all that contradicts it: lies, domination, violence, betrayal and death. Faced with the darkness of Good Friday, the Last Supper is our sacrament of hope. And our sexual behaviour, too, should be more than mutual pleasure. It should form people in mutuality and reciprocity. It should heal wounds and break silence. It should be faithful, giving the time for people to enter more deeply into this risky vulnerability. It should be an act of love, an embodiment of that love which conquers death. And I hope that this does not make me sound too like the Irish bishop who amused everyone because, when he sang the praises of sex, he knew so little!

NOTES

1. Timothy Radcliffe, *What is the Point of Being a Christian?*, Continuum 2005.
2. H. McCabe, *Law, Love and Language*, Continuum 2004, p. 92.
3. Rowan Williams, *The Body's Grace*, written in 1989 for the Lesbian and Gay Christian Movement and available at www.igreens.org.uk/bodys_grace.
4. Ibid.

Part Three

Points of View

Chapter 6

Traces of a Debate, in Fifteen Questions

RETURN TO THE NORMS

Question 1. *Can Eric Fassin spell out his thinking on the question of norms, democracy and the churches?*

Eric Fassin: As everyone knows, the Catholic Church has had some difficulty in reconciling itself with modernity, in particular democratic modernity. Now today the issue is that of an equality in Vatican statements on the collaboration between men and women which shows that it is possible to include a democratic dimension in theological discussion of sexual questions.

So the question is whether the religious authorities choose to continue along a way which today still seems to be preferred, namely stating a law which is based, implicitly or explicitly, on nature, or whether they embrace democracy and try to see what a Christian sexuality would mean if it were accepted in all its logic. In that case the notion of the difference between the sexes might not be a good starting point. But that plays an important role in what the Catholic Church says about the collaboration between men and women. Couldn't we imagine the question of democracy as a starting point?

Clearly, if talk of democracy were thought contrary to religion, that would be the end of the matter. On the other hand, suppose that the Catholic Church tried to use democratic language, as it does in speaking of equality, not just as a concession but in an attempt to rethink, for example, the status of norms. In that case, trying to reflect on establishing a sexuality and sexual order that were fairer could be a programme shared by both lay and religious people.

The alternative is not either to speak of the eternal law based in nature on the difference between the sexes or to say nothing. If there are theologians, it is because everything has not been settled once and for all: the idea that there is still work to do on the respective roles of society and religion does not seem to me to be necessarily anti-religious.

Question 2. *According to the social sciences, the prohibition of incest seems universal. Doesn't that suggest that there are natural laws?*

Eric Fassin: According to Claude Lévi-Strauss in *The Elementary Structures of Kinship* (1949), the universality of the prohibition of incest is fundamental. In the order of culture, in which everything seems variable and only nature seems universal, the prohibition of incest is the only principle which is both social and universal. So some have wanted to see it as a transcendent principle which escapes both history and politics. Lévi-Strauss has been appealed to in support of the assumption that kinship always and everywhere presupposes a father and a mother. So I wrote personally to Lévi-Strauss asking him whether he agreed with this use of his thought and whether I might publish his reply, which I later did. His reply was clear: 'The choices of society are not for the scholar to make *qua* scholar, but for the citizen – and the scholar is also a citizen.' In short, anthropology cannot tell us what we have to do.

A second reply can be given to these hasty readers of anthropology. What in fact is the content of the prohibition of incest? For Lévi-Strauss it is variable: for example, the idea that one must not marry one's sister is not universal (think of ancient Egypt). The church, whose rules about incest have varied since the Middle Ages, is well aware of this. Lévi-Strauss explicitly rejects the idea that the prohibition of incest has a universal content. According to him, the existence of a prohibition is universal, but the definitions of incest vary. The universal is the fact of the rule and not its content.

I would emphasize one point. I did not say that we are moving towards a world without norms or rules, but towards a world whose norms and rules are the object of discussions and negotiations and thus are susceptible to change. To give an example: it seems that the evolution of customs means that today sexual relations between a father-in-law and his daughter-in-law are more than previously seen as incestuous. So we are not seeing a disappearance of prohibitions or an abolition of norms but shifts, reformulations, renegotiations of their content. The question raised is this: in terms of the values that we claim, in what kind of society do we want to live? What norms do we want to defend? Of course we don't all agree, just as we don't all have the same sexuality. All that is normal in a democratic society. Norms no longer impose themselves like evidence; they can be debated.

Question 3. *To give an example, on what is the legal age of consent to sexual relations and to marriage, what one can call sexual coming-of-age, to be based? Can it be based on psychological criteria such as maturity, or physiological criteria such as puberty?*

Eric Fassin: The question is a topical one: what does it mean, basically, that consent is possible at one age and not at another?

A first reading would be psychological: one is mature at one age and not at another. This is hardly satisfying, since we can see that the criterion is arbitrary; for some people maturity never comes and for others it comes very early. Can puberty perhaps be a legal criterion? It could be a legal criterion for the basis of consent, but we know from the existence of paedophilia that there are people who do not respect this criterion. To put it another way, the criterion is not established in nature, since social practices dispute it. So the question is: what do we want to institute socially? That leads us to reflect on the values on which our norms and our laws are based.

If the norms were political and democratic, the condition for consent would be that of being a citizen. In fact one could question the existence of different times of coming of age for voting and for sexual relations, and also for driving a car or going to prison. Why not unify these different times of coming of age and have only one, which implies civic responsibility? The question would arise whether one went by the highest age or the lowest age or took a middle way. I would simply say that to consider 'young people' as citizens wouldn't be a bad idea, at a time when we go on endlessly about their 'civic' responsibility: it's difficult to be a minor and to feel responsible. None of this is immutable: we know that, because the ages for voting and for sexual coming of age have changed in recent decades and the age of criminal responsibility is being discussed. I think that this could be interesting, in the matter of sexuality: the sexual conduct of young people and others would beyond question be more responsible if everyone thought that it involved their responsibility as citizens.

So it is worth taking the trouble to reflect on the very definition of the notion of consent and the criteria on which it should be based. I think that a political criterion rather than psychological criteria should be adopted: we decide by convention that at a given moment people are citizens. There is no absolute reason for saying that one comes of age at eighteen, and we are well aware that plenty of young people have a sexual life before that age.

Certainly that raises the question of the repression of sexual relations between an adult and a minor. In our society we increasingly consider that sexual relations with another person are sexual relations with a true subject. We accept less and less that this can be an impotent subject, in particular a child, not for psychological reasons (that he or she is immature) but for political reasons (that he or she is not a citizen, they are not responsible for their actions). The basic problem is that of recognizing that the question of sexual relations today relates to democracy and that when we have sexual relations it is with other subjects who, like us, are citizens of a democracy whose rights they therefore have.

Question 4. *Doesn't basing laws on democratic debate lead to relativism?*

Eric Fassin: On the contrary, I think that I explicitly criticized relativism. My perspective is a historicist one, and that is different. Historicism does not say that there are no values, but that these are constructed historically. For example, it is clear that today paedophile acts are considered to be far more serious transgressions than they were a century ago. What shocks us has shifted.

Conversely, our society as a whole is less shocked than it was a generation ago by the fact that two men can have sexual relations. These relations appear far less as transgressions – besides, there are those who miss this happy age of transgression. Or again, some forms of sexual violence, including conjugal violence, i.e. violence within the framework of heterosexuality and marriage, are today the object of more censure than they were before. The same goes for the prohibition of incest: what shocks is not given once and for all. We are not seeing norms disappearing, but they are shifting.

BEYOND THE WEST?

Question 5. *Can your discourse be universal? Doesn't it amount to a kind of Western cultural imperialism?*

It seems to me to be valid only in a democracy which allows the discussion of norms. Now today, outside our well-protected Western world, the talk that is most frequently heard is religious talk. Aren't we here among people who confront their analyses and are well aware of them but aren't understood in the wider world? Your suggestion couldn't be heard in a large part of the African continent, or in countries dominated by Islam. For example, on a TV channel in Kinshasa ninety per cent of the speakers are religious, and they speak all day. I don't hear, or rarely hear, the voice of psychologists. Hence the question: what revision of discussions by intellectuals and researchers could give them a hearing in spheres where religious language is evocative and where those who want to discuss norms aren't listened to?

Eric Fassin: My reply will be incomplete: I'm reflecting on this question without feeling that I have the complete answer to it. I work in Africa, on the Ivory Coast and a little in South Africa, and I can see how the problems pose themselves in a different way there. Though South Africa has opened marriage and adoption to same-sex couples, sexual democracy is generally seen in Africa, and also in this country, as a sign of Western decadence. Speaking on the radio about gay marriage to an African public, I took account of the fact that for many of my listeners this was an aberration alien to African culture. Certainly this alien character shouldn't be exaggerated: after all, European psychoanalysts have often reacted in the same way in recent years. Nevertheless, there is a special problem here which relates to the very notion of sexual democracy.

In Europe, I refer back to this democracy because it provides a useful tool for questioning our society. But on the international scene, sexual democracy (and democracy more generally) is talked of less in self-criticism than in the criticism of others: it is a weapon in the international balance of power which has a place in the arsenal of what has to be called imperialism – as when the United States announced women's liberation as an objective when invading Afghanistan. On the other hand, I believe that this sexual imperialism illuminates the phobia of homosexuality, sexual liberation and women's emancipation which is developing in Arab or Muslim countries, notably Egypt. In my view this phobia must be seen less as the heritage of a tradition or the expression of a timeless religion than as a reaction, a form of demarcation from the West. If the West arrogantly affirms that it is the incarnation of modernity, banishing the other (the Muslim in particular) to barbarism, we can see how this other can be tempted to lock itself up in this mirror image. The opposition between 'them' and 'us' that we export encourages some of the 'them' to accept, indeed to exalt, this anti-Western otherness by rejecting everything relating to sexual democracy. So I am not thinking that Africans, for example, are by nature doomed to reproduce a way of talking which resembles that of some conservative intellectuals. It is not a matter of nature but of the historical situation.

That having been said, it is not a matter of resigning oneself to a kind of culturalism which amounts to claiming sexual democracy for 'us' and accepting the order of things among 'them' in order to escape the trap of imperialism. On the other hand, one can at least begin by keeping in mind the critical demand made on 'us' instead of abandoning oneself to the self-satisfaction which people like to show in contrasts with 'them', reflecting that by comparison with the Arab world we are very democratic when it comes to equality and freedom between the sexes and the sexualities.

So when the United States exports secularity, we can ask ourselves, 'How are things in American society?' Isn't the Bush administration opposed to women's rights on its territory, while claiming to impose them elsewhere? And even on the international scene, we can ask questions about a policy which finances projects only if they conform to a view of reproductive health defined over against feminism. It can at least be noted that our demands for equality between the sexes seem stronger when we think of immigrants than when we think of the inequalities in wages and salaries which persist in our society, to take only one example. To put it another way, we can at least begin by criticizing the hypocrisy in our societies. That might perhaps be a way to be heard a bit better when we claim to be teaching others.

NORMS IN THE CHURCH

Question 6. *What can be the origin of norms in a Christian church? How can one reconcile personal behaviour and the doctrine of the church? In particular, what are the positions of the Catholic Church on homosexuality?*

On the question of permissions and prohibitions in sexual behaviour it seems to me that Timothy Radcliffe is suggesting that the Catholic rules are perhaps no longer completely adapted to the situation, that they need to evolve. But what are we to do while we are waiting for that to happen? Is it legitimate to follow our consciences if they tell us that the rule is no longer appropriate, or must we observe the rules in force, in the hope that they will evolve, despite all the difficulties that they entail?

Timothy Radcliffe: The question is a complex one. I think, first, that we must recognize the authority of tradition, but that doesn't mean giving it total authority. In other words, I must take seriously the current teaching of the church, but that doesn't mean that I can't ask questions. We need places for debating within the church, where we can share our questions, our experiences, our attempts, frankly and fearlessly. In my view the priority is to take our reading of the gospel seriously. What Lytta Basset says is fascinating, since she emphasizes that in the end we are there, alone, before God. My reaction is divided: yes, I have to make my decisions, I am face to face with God, with my conscience; no, it is also true that I am never alone, that I belong to the church, to my family, to my brothers.

Lytta Basset: But in the end of the day, after all that, beyond these belongings and what others bring me in the exchanges that I have with them, in the end of the day I find myself alone before God.

Timothy Radcliffe: In the end I find myself in the kingdom of God!

Question 7. *When two persons of the same sex love each other with love, understanding and agreement, when they are in a relationship of truth of heart, body, mind, how can one talk of sin?*

Timothy Radcliffe: In a sense you're asking what sin is, and I can't answer that question easily. Honestly, I don't know. I think that if the church wants to achieve a deeper sexual ethic, it must not only speak but also listen. A cardinal said that there are three authorities in the church. First of all, there is the authority of tradition, of the gospel and of doctrine, which relates above all to the responsibility of the hierarchy. Secondly, there is reason, which is involved above all in discussions, debates, universities. This cardinal adds a third authority, that of experience. To construct a theology of sexuality we need these three authorities, whereas often we think only of the authority of tradition and the hierarchy, and we don't want to listen to the authority of experience.

For example, the church is full of homosexuals who have prayed, who have had deep experiences over the years, and I don't think that we could have an ethic that commands attention if we haven't listened to their experience. That's the next step in the reflection that we're talking about here. I think in particular of a homosexual couple, friends of mine, Catholics. They've struggled and prayed for twenty-seven years. The church hasn't simply to tell them what to do; it must listen to their experiences.

So I just don't know. I clearly see the need for every human being to express his or her tenderness. One can't be human if one doesn't have the possibility of receiving and giving one's body naturally to another. We need this, since we aren't pure spirits, angels. There aren't many angels here and now – perhaps some hidden ones. The first thing is to listen.

AROUND THE DIFFERENCE

Question 8. *Can one advocate an absence of hierarchy and equality between the sexes while recognizing that there are differences between them?*

Eric Fassin: Does renouncing hierarchy mean effacing the difference? Or conversely, can one have equality in difference? To answer this question I shall turn it round: what does recognize mean here? To institute it by law? Do we want, today, by our laws, not only to recognize that there are both men and women – that is written into the civil state, even if not everyone finds their place easily in this binary structure – but to give them different rights? We can see how our laws tend to move away from this differential treatment, for example with paternity leave (and not just maternity leave). Likewise, it is not identical with having such and such a sexuality or sexual identity. There are considerable variations in practices and portrayals, not only between homosexuals and heterosexuals (not to mention all those who find it difficult to fit into this binary structure), but also in the very different ways of expressing these sexualities or sexual orientations.

The question remains: do we want to introduce these differences and thus investigate them by means of the law and more generally by normative prescriptions deriving from the churches, schools, learned discussions, etc.? That amounts to saying that it is desirable to preserve them, indeed to emphasize them. In short, do we want to introduce the differences and thus harden them by assigning laws and norms – or can we perhaps leave room for free social interplay in order to give more encouragement to collective and individual adjustments in matters of this kind (the way to express masculinity or femininity) and in sexuality (the way to express different sexual orientations)? A real battle is going on here today.

Let's take an example. I wouldn't presume that all those whom I'm addressing here have the same sexuality. For all that, is it necessary to divide up the auditorium by such a criterion – the heterosexuals on the right, the homosexuals on the left, the bisexuals in the middle, those who are continent, chaste or 'asexual' at the back? We can see that at the same time these differences mark inequalities: those who are at the back might perhaps demand to be in the front row.

Granted, no one says that they want to institute a hierarchy, but in practice we are in the process of establishing a hierarchy between the sexualities when we say, for example, 'Marriage is too important to open it up to same-sex couples' – and that is being said today. From this point of view it seems to me that there is a state homophobia. That is not to say that people themselves are homophobic. They can be open, tolerant, sympathetic, but when one institutes a hierarchy of sexualities, saying implicitly or explicitly that heterosexuality is better, and tests it by reserving for it the institutions which are considered most precious, such as marriage and the family, one is instituting homophobia on the part of the state and the law.

Let's compare this with racial questions. In 1896 a decision by the Supreme Court of the United States on the segregation of the sexes was justified by the assertion that Blacks and Whites can be equal while being separated. In 1954, another decree of the same court reversed the argument. How does that relate to sexual questions today? Must we remain in the logic of segregation or support desegregation? Beyond question some people are disturbed at the lack of differentiation between the sexes and sexualities. I, though, am more disturbed by a state of tension over the idea, which for me is not very democratic, that segregation is not a barrier to equality.

Question 9. *Lytta Basset emphasizes the importance of the call for differentiation in the Bible, in particular in the first three chapters of Genesis. Does the gospel emphasize this as much as the Old Testament?*

Lytta Basset: Yes, the gospel is also very disturbing when it speaks of hatred, as when Jesus says: 'It is not peace that I have come to bring but the sword. For I have come to set son against father, daughter against mother, daughter-in-law against mother-in law.' It says that in the text.

Question 10. *What is the connection with the difference between the sexes, that primordial physiological fact in some anthropological* *or psychoanalytic discussions? Must talk of respecting the other, without fusion, be understood as applying just to the couple, man and woman, or does it also apply to a homosexual couple who love each other truly?*

Lytta Basset: To my mind it applies from A to Z; it's the same thing, and I could have spelt that out more.

Question 11. *It's very difficult to speak to young people of lack, of separation, of distance, and the same goes for tenderness. One talks of these things very rapidly and sometimes in a very superficial way. Can something else also be done?*

Lytta Basset: It seems to me that young people experience lack, separation and even abandonment in all kinds of ways and that that can be painful. We must grasp these occasions to engage in dialogue, from where they are. Certainly, they aspire to fusion, but at the same time they see clearly that this doesn't work. It's from that point that it's interesting to speak, to share with them, to educate, to make them understand that this is a completely normal process of differentiation. If through these exchanges they manage to live out this process without being demolished by it, they can grow and become more aware of what they are, of their identity. Certainly the key word is support, being with them, supporting young people in this process.

LOVE IN THE TIME OF AIDS

Question 12. *Timothy Radcliffe has spoken of love and sexuality. He says that making love is transmitting the gift, is* *being human, that love is stronger than death, is a promise of life and forgiveness, taking the risk of being touched by the other. But there is also AIDS, and suddenly all these phrases take on another connotation. How does AIDS modify these portrayals of the gift associated with love? What are we to say to those who live with the virus and who want to encounter the other, yet who fear transmitting AIDS, or being super-contaminated?*

The Catechism of the Church *says that sexuality is a blessing. It has been said here that sexuality is not summed up in procreation, that there is also the sense of an encounter with the other and a giving without reserve. The fact remains that the virus raises a barrier: one cannot give oneself without reserve, one has to set up a barrier for the safety of the other.*

Timothy Radcliffe: In the end, when facing AIDS the challenges are those that everyone experiences. Sexuality, tenderness in relationships, can also be a sign that love is stronger than death. I've experienced moving moments with people who are dying of AIDS and I've seen that in these moments a kiss, a touch, tenderness, remain a sign of hope. It's a sign of hope even between those who have AIDS: death doesn't have the last word. In fact the issues are the same: how to speak by touching, how to express communion through physical and even sexual contact. It's clear that there are limits. One mustn't be a danger to the other. But I think one can practise all this with an incarnate hope and tenderness, since transcendence is expressed in history. Christianity is a religion of incarnation. It is here in our bodies that we must live out our faith with one another.

Yesterday evening I went with a friend to an exhibition

on melancholia. What impressed me was how melancholia, which is a state of mind, was expressed by the body. It was fascinating to see how every exhibit depicting melancholia gave it a physical manifestation, above all with the hands, which are always central in this kind of portrayal. Even love which is truly spiritual, truly pure in this sense, needs physical expression. I am a religious and have made a vow of chastity, but that doesn't imply that my loving relations with others must be purely mental. We all need physical contacts, and these contacts can be of different kinds. Sexuality is far more varied than the one complete sexual relation. It is everywhere; when we are present, when we see one another, when we touch one another, when we are in the presence of the other. In this sense, even for someone who carries the virus, though a total physical relationship may pose a problem, love can penetrate all one's sexuality.

Lytta Basset: Many women have had children and at a given moment have no longer been able to have them. They have no longer been able to bear a child and know that they wouldn't be capable of adopting one. It is then that the anguish of being pregnant appears. Here we are talking about other anguishes, less serious at first sight, but which in some cases nevertheless give an impression of total impossibility. In my view the condom is something of the same order; it's a limit, at all events something necessary for the quality of life one wants to have.

Question 13. *I knew a Ugandan priest who lived with HIV for fifteen years. He had an incredible ministry which made a deep*

89

impression in many countries. Here is an example of someone who lived positively with HIV, who was a Christian and even a priest, and who showed by his life that being HIV positive doesn't prevent one from remaining active and productive and having a great deal of influence. In the relationship of the reciprocal gift represented by a sexual relationship, isn't the greatest obstacle the fear of AIDS, more than AIDS itself, since there are concrete means of prevention?

Timothy Radcliffe: The English Dominicans began to get involved in the problem of AIDS twenty years ago, after reading an article on a young man struck by the virus. The nurses were so afraid of the illness that they didn't dare enter his room: they left the food outside and he had to get out of bed to go and get it. In 1985 that caused such a shock that people began to think differently. This story shows how right you are. Fear is the great enemy, the great enemy of love. We must encourage one another.

AND VIOLENCE?

Question 14. *Lytta Basset asserts that even in violent sexual relationships the self of the other is never destroyed. From hearsay experience I'm afraid that children who have been raped by parents have a part of their 'self' which is very difficult to rebuild.*

Lytta Basset: I've a little tip relating to the difficulty of rebuilding. Experience tells me that it's possible to have repeated for years, 'I'm so destroyed that I could never reshape myself, never get on my feet, etc.' This is also the experience of those who provide support. We see people whose lives, whose pasts, whose childhoods have really been devastated, but there is something deep down which makes them fight – of course assuming that the person at any rate has a minimal desire to live. I agree, that takes a great deal of time, sometimes decades. But where the person has lost all courage, I can't deny that this happens.

Question 15. *I understand, but I've also witnessed the brutality of sex. I see young people who can't love as they want because the group constrains them. It's a weakness to love in some difficult neighbourhoods. One could also talk of the development of the 'bareback' phenomenon (the choice to make love without protection), of the initiation of young people often through pornographic films without any emotional life, of cybersex, etc. What transition is there between what unites us today, which is very beautiful, and this reality which is sometimes hell?*

Timothy Radcliffe: This question, too, is very difficult. First of all we must be present in these places. I feel that you are already there, and that's magnificent, it's a blessing for us, for if we don't share lives and suffering, if we don't know the brutalities that these young people have to endure every day, we can't do anything. I've often been amazed to see how small Christian communities are present in the most abysmal, the most suffering places. We Christians must also be present in the media, in the production of films, in virtual reality, not to make propaganda but as a presence of the church and of Christ, in order to try to share a sweeter vision of Christianity. The most important thing is not to keep aloof. In that way we preserve hope among these young people who are so wounded, since our little experience, in Europe or elsewhere, shows that the temptation when people are imprisoned in a negative perception of themselves is to despair. That's a type of hell. We have to be there with them, with our hope.

Chapter 7

View from Africa

Abdon Goudjo

The reflections in this book are formulated within the terms of reference of Western societies. Deliberately, we have not taken account of the global diversity of forms of Christianity or of their relations to sexuality in other cultures: for this first attempt, such a task seemed impossible. However, because sub-Saharan Africa is so important in the AIDS epidemic, as are the campaigns that 'Christians & AIDS' is carrying on there, an African has been asked to react to the remarks made by the other contributors.

I want to bear witness not only as a doctor, but also in the light of my Christian training. In fact I happen to be the nephew of an old archbishop of Cotonou in Benin and the brother of a priest of the same diocese. This context explains why the three voices which you have just heard put demanding questions to me. Questions are also raised by my brother, who is a priest, in connection with the prevention of HIV: their background is the teaching of the Catholic Church centred on concepts of abstinence and fidelity. The over-cautiousness of this church on the issue of prevention is all the more surprising when in

Benin the church is heavily involved in medical, social and nutritional care of men and women living with HIV and those close to them. This is happening within the framework of the Sedekon ('with the heart') project in Abomey (Davougon), Parakou (Saint-Jean de Boko) and other regions of the Congo. But on the issue of primary and above all secondary care (i.e. care of those who are HIV positive) the church continues to keep harping on its rigid teaching.

Given this fact, we must return to the content and form of the campaigns of prevention in order to encourage responsible reflection and behaviour among those on whom they are focused. In prevention it is important to help people to reflect and to support them in an approach which is appropriate to their situation, rather than to try at all costs to convince them by slogans and injunctions, 'it must be' and 'there is only'.

What can we offer those who are HIV positive? Once they have got over the news that they are HIV positive, with the pain, fear, anxiety and despair which follow, they gradually regain a foothold in life, sexual life in particular. Are we only to propose sexual abstinence, since even in the case of a couple both of whom are contaminated, fidelity does not mean that over-contamination is avoided? Certainly these people have a mind which one can stimulate by recommending abstinence, but they also have a body. Let's remember the words of the gospel: 'The spirit is willing, but the flesh is weak.' That means that it is a good thing for the Catholic Church to maintain the principles of abstinence and fidelity; but it is also useful for it to have other views on what means of prevention are suitable for certain situations and, among other things, for it to be able to suggest the use of condoms. However, I'm afraid that this isn't the case. When it comes to secondary prevention some members of the clergy are quite uncomfortable about the difficulties people have with the teaching of their church, so without explicitly promoting condoms, they refer to one of the Ten Commandments ('Thou shalt not kill'), thus leaving it to their flock to disentangle a very enigmatic message. For that reason, even if I always see myself as being at the heart of the church, from time to time I disagree with it. I see, I come across, too much suffering. Those who have spoken on other pages of this book are sending many messages to all the churches, to all pastors. We need to take another look at the pastoral care of patients, the HIV positive, couples only one of which has HIV.

I shall now react to what has been said so far, in order to relate it to the prevention of HIV. Timothy Radcliffe begins with Christ's words, 'This is my body given for you.' This is my body. What is this body? An abstinent body? A faithful body? A protected body? And how do we fill out these terms? Today in every African country the posters on the walls contain three words. If you go to Bobo-Dioulasso you see 'Fidelity, Abstinence, Condom', if you go to Brazzaville you see 'Abstinence, Fidelity, Condom', if you return to Cotonou you see 'Abstinence . . .' Let's revisit this trio. What meaning do we give to the three words?

ABSTINENCE?

There are some who abstain voluntarily. That is their choice and that is their right. Why shouldn't some people have taken a vow of chastity? What interests me as a doctor of public health is what happens when abstinence stops. For abstinence lasts only during the time of abstinence. The majority of human beings who have decided to be abstinent don't succeed in remaining abstinent in the long run. So it's good to have alternative ways of coping with the problem and another approach to prevention, which presupposes the acquisition of other reflexes. It's good to reflect with those concerned on situations of risk and an individualized plan for reducing risks. For example, suppose I don't succeed in practising the abstinence to which I am committed by my faith or my ideal of life? What should I do if I fail? Must I both transgress and take risks? Or though I am transgressing, must I protect myself at the same time?

In my conversations with some religious about providing information and becoming sensitive to the prevention of AIDS, I leave to them the task of speaking of the ideal of faith or life. I present my contribution as an alternative for those who do not succeed in living out this ideal: I tell them about what one can do in everyday life as frail human beings.

FIDELITY?

I like Timothy Radcliffe's comments on idealized fidelity in connection with the fidelity of the couple: it is a perfect fidelity. But I link them with the words of Lytta Basset: 'Fidelity to oneself is often more important than fidelity to the other.' Is this fidelity that is recommended – 'I will never leave my spouse' – a fidelity to oneself?

But must fidelity of the heart, of the mind, also be a fidelity of the body? To take an example: in my personal situation and because of professional commitments, I travel a lot. Now those who travel a lot see the number of their social relationships increase with the risk, or the opportunity, for intimate, indeed sexual, relationships. Clearly commitment to fidelity of the body is affected by this. At the level of health, travellers must see to their own protection, but over and above that, what about the protection of the loved ones who are waiting for them? The notion of fidelity isn't as easy as the slogans on walls suggest. Fidelity for whom? Fidelity how? There are probably variations of this notion of fidelity. It's good for the church, for all the churches, to revisit this concept and give us some reflections on it. The slogans have their limitations.

Here's another situation: the sex professionals. In the Rex district of Pointe-Noire there are numerous women leaning against walls, about one every ten metres, offering their services for part of the night. What message are we to give them? Certainly they aren't abstinent; they have no bodily fidelity, but they have fidelities of the heart. They have their 'loves'. These loves are the ones with whom they have sexual relations which are always unprotected. So they have a certain fidelity: they say, 'It's my man! Everyone in the district knows that.' On the other hand, there is the client who approaches and tries to negotiate a price. The negotiation is as banal as anywhere else on the planet. At what price will the matter of prevention arise? At less than two euros, the lowest price, the majority of women will refuse unprotected sexual relations; if the client suggests twice as much, they may still resist his proposal; at ten euros they begin to reflect; at forty euros even those with the best training find it hard to resist, since this is equivalent to at least twenty clients. Given all this, they ask us, 'Find us another way of being able to go on resisting.' We've told them: 'Form a group. As soon as a man begins this sordid game of negotiating, gang up and chase him away.' Clearly this presupposes strong solidarity. So when they get to know one another well they learn to become real agents of prevention, so that the client who approaches them does not disturb the equilibrium of the group. Of course they could change their job – and we could help them to do so. Why not? But for the moment, they carry on with their job and ask us to help them to protect themselves better.

CONDOM?

This example shows us that the condom by itself isn't an absolute answer to the prevention of the risk of HIV. Let's also analyse this. The condom is only an instrument too. The important thing is the right moment to negotiate it. In the work that I'm doing at present in Brazzaville, we've learned that the majority of young women who suggest a condom once they are in the room with a partner are already in danger of submitting to his will. The same also goes most frequently for married women, who are economically dependent on their husbands. In both cases, as agents of public health, we have to teach them to negotiate the condom before entering the room, in other words, from the time when the partner or spouse indicates the possibility of a sexual relationship. For example, we invite women to reflect on the significance of an invitation to a bar or to dinner. If they want a condom to be used, it is at this stage that they must learn to negotiate it. Once in the room, the woman who brings out a condom which her companion hasn't been prepared for, or which he doesn't agree to, is exposed to violent reactions: physical and/or sexual violence.

So we lead women to reflect on situations which generate risks, in order to allow them to anticipate the best way of protecting themselves. For example, if you know that it's risky to enter such and such a bar, you can learn to avoid going there. However, you're never protected from the unforeseen. I'm thinking of a young man who recently came for a consultation and told me, 'I went into a club restaurant (a *nganga*) with my condoms in their wrappers.' But the unfortunate person drank a beer, then two, three or four, and of course when he had made a conquest 'the condoms remained in their wrappers'. In other words, when it comes to reducing risks, there is an enormous amount of work to be done, despite the promotion of the condom. All the approaches to prevention have weaknesses, hence the importance of providing support.

SEXUALITY AND POVERTY

These testimonies have come out of my African experiences. For all that, there is no specifically African reading of the prevention of AIDS. That's universal quite simply because it's addressed to all human beings.

That's why I value Lytta Basset's comments on otherness. On every continent the relationship with the other is absolutely precious. But what relationship to the other does a destitute young single mother have when, in order to have the euros necessary to feed her child, she is driven to negotiate a sexual relationship? It's all very complex. By contrast, the context of my preventative work is specifically African. One doesn't achieve prevention on the basis of theoretical considerations but starting from the concrete situations in which Africans find themselves.

On this continent, the churches and mosques are probably the institutions which most people frequent, more people than I will ever meet in the place I have in Brazzaville. In this part of Central Africa one hundred per cent of the inhabitants are said to belong to a religion: ninety per cent are Christian, with all the variants of Christianity. The Catholics have ceased to be the most numerous, and the word of the Pope is no longer the most influential word in Congo-Brazzaville. One hears the 'revivalist' churches most often. They are thought to be influenced by American Protestantism and rely on important financial gifts from PEPFAR, the American programme against AIDS. Now, of the fifteen billion dollars from PEPFAR, a third is devoted to the promotion, backed up by religious personalities, of abstinence before marriage and then fidelity between the couple. In almost every district you will find the hut of one of these religious personalities. When a grand master whom they call 'apostle' or 'pastor' presents himself, advertising streamers appear, like those for football matches: 'The apostle will receive this evening from 16.00 to 23.00 . . .' Very few churches in the traditional Protestant sphere are capable of bringing together so many people; the Catholic Church can no longer do so. So there is new work to be done. Here perhaps we have the phenomenon described by Eric Fassin of the imperialism of a democracy using a religious intermediary. It's an element which is very difficult to take into account.

The churches which talk coherently about combating AIDS have begun to organize. They have created a collective, COREC (Collective of Religious Organizations of the Congo). Though I have reservations about the effectiveness of preventive actions against HIV in Africa, I become more optimistic when I see these very dynamic churches in place. One of the best centres for the care of the sick in Brazzaville, the Mayangui Centre, belongs to the Evangelical Church of the Congo. I appreciate the fact that it receives everyone, without proselytism. It makes suggestions about preventing AIDS, leaving people considerable freedom of choice and offering them real support. It's good that the churches are being involved in this kind of service. That's another aspect of my African experience.

Unfortunately all these reflective approaches to sexuality which seek to develop individual responsibility are thwarted in countries with few resources, since the economic aspect is important and disturbs everything. For me, the question of 'Christians and sexuality' isn't the most important one. Unfortunately the most important questions are 'poverty and health', 'poverty and sexuality'. If I engage in a reflection with a religious approach, there is a level of poverty below which people don't hear what I say. *A fortiori*, I don't hear what I love to hear in Europe, in a debate in which I enjoy being involved. For while these reflections may stimulate the mind if they allow me to enrich my ideas and my words and through me to enrich the local churches with which I work, they also bring out the great gap that I see on the ground. That's my testimony. I don't want it to be pessimistic but incisive and direct, and I offer it as food for thought.

Chapter 8

Conclusion: A Christian Contribution to an Ethic of Sexuality

Antoine Lion

This is an attempt to think about old questions in a new context. I want to locate it in two millennia of relations between Christianity and sexuality, then in the changes of recent decades, and finally in the 'time of AIDS'. I shall then explain the genesis of this book and finally, without seeking to synthesize remarks which are enriched by their very diversity, I shall indicate some sources of light for the time to come.

A HISTORICAL SURVEY

First of all, the three terms around which I shall gravitate here date from different times. 'Christians' is a title that is twenty centuries old, a term denoting the first disciples of Christ in Antioch according to the Acts of the Apostles; 'sexuality' is a linguistic creation of the 1840s, which only assumed its present meaning in the twentieth century;

'AIDS' dates from 1981. When speaking of 'sexuality' I shall guard against any anachronism and against tacking on to quite different contexts the reality that the word denotes. Body, flesh, life, being married or virgin, are the words with which the realities which concern us have been formulated at other times.

IN THE LONG RUN

At the beginning of Christianity, two models appear in the works attributed to St Paul. According to the first of his writings, composed while impatiently awaiting the imminent return of the Lord, these times are the last in a world which is destined to disappear. People must detach themselves from its realities. The best thing is to abstain from marrying if one is not yet married, or if one is married to refrain from carnal relations. This was not to pass a negative judgement on sexual life but to recall the only thing that counted: to prepare for the return of the Lord. 1 Corinthians clearly affirms this.

Time passed, the Lord did not return and the world did not disappear. So it was necessary to 'redeem the time'. The ideal of monogamous marriage – not evident at the time – commended itself. One text articulates this conception, the Letter to the Ephesians, attributed to St Paul but from another hand than his. Here conjugal union becomes the sign of the covenant of God with believers: 'Husbands, love your wives as Christ loved his church.' One cannot attach a higher significance to marriage, even if it was not recognized as a sacrament until the thirteenth century in practice and the sixteenth century in Catholic dogma.

Of these two models anchored in the New Testament, the most eminent remained virginal celibacy, adopted by those men and women who embraced the monastic life, and after that the different forms of the 'religious life'. Not without difficulty, celibacy was imposed on the clergy who shaped the thought of the church. The legitimate field of sexuality was defined: at best virginity; failing that, marriage. Any other practice was in contravention of the divine laws and was steeped in sin, and that ruled out words other than those of rejection, judgement and a call for conversion. In this domain nothing was venial, everything was serious. So we note a long lack of thought about anything that escaped the two models: a traditional deficiency which for the most part lies at the beginning of our current difficulties.

To begin with, this Christianity spread in a culture dominated by Greece. Plato's disciples professed a dualism of soul and body, alien to Hebrew thought. While this dualism rejected the excesses of Manichaeism, it invited disparagement of the body. With a theological language formulated by men and primarily for men, it was also the foundation for a basic inequality between the two sexes. In short, while femininity was certainly called to salvation, it remained bound up with sin. Thus theology and culture reinforced each other in a basic accord.

Recent decades

Let's centre for a moment on the Catholic Church in the Western world, where the changes have been most visible: things were different in the Protestant and Orthodox churches. In 1962, at the opening of the Second Vatican

Council, the bishops had the freedom to discuss all the topics they thought necessary. After four years of their work, the council fathers saw only two topics withdrawn: contraception, the study of which was entrusted in 1964 by the Pope to a commission, and then, in 1965, the celibacy of priests. The Pope reserved to himself the right to decide directly on these matters.

At that time contraception was the important topic, since new techniques and the ease of using them had revolutionized its social use. After long reflection, in 1968 Paul VI promulgated the encyclical *Humanae vitae*, reaffirming vigorously the traditional bans. Since numerous couples thought that in all conscience they could not apply these rules, discreet and massive dissent set in among Catholics. Moreover certain episcopates opened up a way for such couples, referring to a conscience clause which allowed dissent with the words of the Pope. That was no longer the case with John-Paul II, who affirmed that the 'ethical norm' in substance 'is not a doctrine invented by God': it has been inscribed by the creative hand of God in the very nature of the human person. 'Hence it does not allow any exception: no personal or social circumstance has ever been able to justify such an act, it cannot nor will it be able to do so in the future.'

In Western societies, other cracks began to appear around the Roman doctrines. The vast increase in the number of couples living together before asking for marriage no longer met solely with disapproval. The ban on any medically assisted procreation, including that between spouses, was difficult to understand; after the rejection of childless sex, this was a rejection of the child without sex, even if the reasons behind both practices are very different.

When the behaviour of a vast majority takes no account of established norms (though some have been established only since the nineteenth century), there is some grandeur in simply reiterating them. However, this practice clashes with the very ancient doctrine of 'reception' which is required if a proposition of the church is to be considered valid. In contemporary terms, the Jesuit psychoanalyst and philosopher Michel de Certeau said that any procedure which maintains principles regardless of practices 'clashes with an essential postulate of modernity, namely the decisive character of practices in the development of the theory which articulates them and which they verify or falsify'. The Catholic magisterium has often thought it its duty to confront the culture of its time. To do this on a point which is not evidently at the heart of the proclamation of the gospel has a consequence, namely a loss of credibility, not only for the precise subject but for the very institution which holds the principle.

The time of AIDS

When the epidemic struck, no one foresaw a new shock. However, a strange misunderstanding fixed itself on a particular object, the condom. The use of condoms was officially rejected, since they are prohibited to a legitimate couple as a means of contraception. Did the official authorities of the church grasp that this object was no longer regarded as an obstacle to the transmission of life but as protection against a possible transmission of death? They seemed to insist on the rejection of a means, without seeing that its goal had been reversed.

No one criticized the reminder of traditional teaching in what the magisterium said about prevention. Those who conformed appreciated being supported and encouraged in this difficult way. But that was not the case for the majority: people either admired this ideal without succeeding in putting it into practice or lived differently, as did homosexuals, among others.

This reminder often went hand in hand with a discrediting of other means of prevention. So in the eyes of many people the main concern of the Catholic magisterium seemed to be to defend its traditional positions. A contradiction developed: whereas Christians often found themselves in the front line in caring and taking charge, especially in Africa, the Catholic Church seemed to be a brake on the indispensable struggle against the global epidemic.

In the West, another tension related to homosexuality. Homosexuals were both the first to be affected and the first to engage in powerful initiatives against the scourge. Their image was transformed: homosexuality was no longer only a personal reality, but took on the collective dimension of a social fact. However, at the end of 1986, at a time when gay milieus were being ravaged by the epidemic, the 'Letter to the Bishops of the Catholic Church on the Pastoral Care of Homosexual Persons', signed by Cardinal Ratzinger, spoke of the inclination to homosexuality as an 'objective disorder' and ignored AIDS, as, with all the more reason, it ignored the role of homosexuals in the struggle. In the years which followed, numerous positions were adopted by Christians. In particular it was emphasized that the epidemic was not just a problem of health but a social and political question, and some adopted vigorous positions against any exclusion and stigmatization of those affected.

The fact remains that, confronted with new situations, the Catholic Church found itself subjected to twofold and apparently contradictory criticism. It was accused of talking too much, of rejecting methods of prevention which were recognized to be necessary (even if a number of authorized voices tempered this point of view) and harshly judging homosexuals, who were effective agents in the struggle against the virus and were themselves sorely tried. Another criticism thought that in other spheres this church no longer seemed capable of offering a word that could be heard. The treasures represented by its immense spiritual, symbolic and ethical resources, its reserves of meaning for times of trial, seemed to have become unavailable.

A movement, a book

The 'Christians & AIDS' association, which is primarily ecumenical, came into being in 1990. After fifteen years of work, with its freedom and collective experience, helped by competences from elsewhere, it is engaging publicly in the kind of reflection presented in this book.

To understand better, for a moment let's substitute elementary geometry for history. Think of a triangle the apexes of which are the three terms in the title of this book. Let's call them A ('Christians'), B ('sexuality') and

C ('AIDS'). In any triangle one can link two of the apexes in three ways, distinguishing them from the third. So 'A and C, opposite B', will be our starting point. Then we shall look at 'B and C, opposite A' (I shall say 'viewed from A'). Finally we shall discuss 'A and B, opposite C' ('in the time of C'), where we shall rediscover the title of the book. Let me explain.

'A and C/B': Christians and AIDS/opposite sexuality

At the end of the 1980s, women and men struck in various ways by an epidemic which was then in its most murderous phase decided to work together. To give a name to their association, between the words 'Christians' and 'AIDS' they put the sign '&', the typographical ampersand, to support their improbable venture.

Rarely have such diverse people joined together: professionals working in health (carers, agents of public health, researchers), in the social sector (urban districts, the prisons, drug addicts), in education (school nurses, teachers, school heads), in the activities of the churches (hospital or prison almoners, pastors, theologians); militant members of associations, recent ones such as AIDES, and older ones such as 'David and Jonathan'; and, of course people affected by the virus in their own lives or the lives of friends, living or dead: parents, friends, relatives, children. One could be in one or other of these categories, indeed in all at once. In addition, everyone called themselves Christians, whatever their church, or felt concerned about the future of Christianity. So we found this nurse and this monk, this sick person and this journalist, this university lecturer and this religious, these parents caring for a sick child or even in mourning, this African priest and this drug addict, this psychoanalyst and this computer scientist, this grandmother and this musician, embarking on the same movement, committed to common action. The network spread. Local groups multiplied, up to forty. Several objectives brought them together: one of these was to reflect and to help reflection.

Now the question of sexuality arose, something that concerns everyone except little children in this epidemic. Some of us encountered homosexuality for the first time. Moreover the Christian homosexuals of 'David and Jonathan' had proposed the first dossier of reflections on AIDS in 1988. In addition there was the turmoil of some parents when a son suddenly announced his HIV contamination and his homosexuality, if this had previously been hidden. Christian circles were no more spared these shocks than others. Some families experienced this thunderclap in a dramatic way, to the point of refusing, at least for a time, to have their child at home. We have seen cases when the news of the sickness appeared more acceptable than that of the sexual orientation. More often, however, this trial produced unexpected openings.

In short, questions and attitudes in the sphere of sexuality have been at the heart of the life of 'Christians & AIDS'. We needed to go further.

'B and C/A': sexuality and AIDS/viewed by Christians

Among its missions, the young association felt called to contribute to the effort of prevention. Learning that Christians were involved in the struggle against the epidemic, confessional schools appealed to local groups.

Some of us formed in response to the demand. It seemed normal to remind people of received morality, Catholic morality in particular, to speak of abstinence outside marriage and fidelity. This reminder was sometimes well received; the drama being played out seemed to confirm how well-founded these virtues were. If everyone practised them, the scourge would soon be over. Thus the relevance of traditional doctrine seemed reinforced, above all if it was coupled – which it was – with unconditional care of those who were suffering. In the face of them, every form of exclusion and rejection had to be fought against. But this wasn't so simple.

Thus in the schools many young people, dissatisfied with such assumptions, questioned the new teachers of prevention about modes of protection. Teachers had to reply to questions such as, 'Sir, what do you think about condoms?', or, more confused (this was a pupil in the fourth form), 'Miss, is making love without a condom a sin?' In the many public debates organized by 'Christians & AIDS', other comments kept coming up. We were told that many of us had to equip ourselves with new competences. Without playing the role of doctor when one wasn't, without claiming skills of organizations such as the AIDS Information Serivice, it was important to learn and reflect. An anthropological, ethical, indeed theological way of thinking was required. So training became a priority for the organization and internal debate one of its practices.

One episode was decisive for me. I had invited the founder of the AIDS Information Service to a meeting of the association in 1995; he was one of the chief figures in the struggle against the virus, which was soon to carry him off. He spoke of one of his friends, a homosexual, sick and in hospital, who knew that he was close to death. Far removed from any church, after much hesitation and to the surprise of those close to him, he asked to see a priest. The hospital chaplain, who came quickly, listened to him and said, 'Repent, and God will welcome you.' The relationship thereupon went sour and the sick man went to his end in great bitterness.

The story shook the meeting. I murmured to myself the words of St John of the Cross on the theologians of his time: 'They do not know how to tell me what I want.' Didn't this priest know that at the heart of Christianity is the proclamation of the love of God for everyone? The word of hope comes first. It opens up a way on which one can discover God's mercy and also shows that one lacks his love; it is a stage, it is not the threshold. And that has nothing to do with forms of sexuality, but with the quality of relationships with others. The chaplain lacked judgement, but had he been helped to face the changes taking place? This story reinforced us in the conviction that, modestly, 'Christians & AIDS' had to work to make the Christian attitude on sexuality more in keeping with the gospel; we had to land without fear on new shores.

One doesn't plunge into such questions without feeling more or less concerned, without asking oneself also about the Christian attitude to sexuality in general. The title of this book took shape – and touched on the third relationship of our triangle.

'A and B/C': Christians and sexuality/in the time of AIDS

The re-reading of Christian traditions did not allow an

easy response to all the questions which emerged. In the threat and the presence of AIDS, mixed up with so many stories of lives turned upside down, we had to think again about part of what we had received, to disengage what abides and discern what has to be discovered. The idea – trivial in itself – of a colloquium to advance reflection developed. For two years, a working party defined the objectives, refined the theme, and chose the methods, which meant combining two approaches.

We invited some people from outside the movement. They were the trio whose voices readers have heard, chosen for their competence and their diversity: one woman and two men; or two foreigners (Swiss, English) and one French; or a theologian, a theologian psychoanalyst and a sociologist.

We also undertook to take up what was being said in the association in its diversity, to give words to what was known, experienced and thought by its members, to pass from impression to expression. A broad consultation, made through local groups, ended in June 2005 with a whole day of sessions, attended by some shrewd observers. Another semester allowed the preparation of the colloquium on which some of this book is based. Finally came the work of preparing the book itself, which is not meant to consist of off-putting 'minutes', but to be a summing up, provisional and open, of reflection in progress.

Its formulations are not immutable but provisional and, we hope, stimulating. The collection brought together here contains comforting or disturbing words, depending on the case, positions matured in the cauldron of shared work or testimonies to often painful experiences, encounters between theological and spiritual traditions with a reality that is heard and experienced, reactions to the debate, an echo from Africa. Every reader can draw his or her own conclusions about the way forward. Now I shall risk formulating mine: what have I got out of the present work of reflection?

LIGHT ON THE WAY

A shift in references

Timothy Radcliffe refuses to be imprisoned in the discussion about permission and prohibition and to link sexuality only with reproduction. Beyond that, he engages in a positive discussion which is both traditional and new. To do this he takes his starting point from the Gospel narrative of the Last Supper, in the course of which, against the dark horizon of the passion, Jesus signifies the Passover that he is on the point of celebrating. We can read here a Christian conception of sexuality in terms of gift, of truth, of the rejection of violence, of communion, of fidelity and of life. Timothy Radcliffe attests that not only does the Eucharist illuminate sexuality, but the opposite is also true. Our experience of the gift of the body refines our view of the gift that the Lord gives, and a right sexual relationship can say something about the gospel in the world. These remarks give human sexuality a new dignity and beauty.

With other words, Lytta Basset also rejects any definition of what must or must not take place between two human beings who love each other. In thinking about sexuality, with her biblical knowledge and her clinical experience she has chosen to speak of the couple, in whom what allows agreement of hearts and bodies is found. Each is alone before God, yet human existence is accomplished in a partnership, the authentic criteria of which Lytta Basset discerns. Fidelity is primarily to oneself before being fidelity towards others. The biblical narrative of the creation of man and woman emphasizes that the principle of otherness and the responsibility that it implies comes before the distinction between the two sexes, and is thus open to any type of couple. Thus sexuality finds its spiritual basis and authentic partnership taking on a divine dimension.

These two suggestions are liberating. They seem to me to offer Christians, in different styles, new points of reference for thinking about sexuality in its riches and perhaps living it out in a way more in keeping with the gospel. Nevertheless, it will be noted that in the face of some formidable questions, Timothy Radcliffe responds with modesty, repeating that he does not have all the solutions, that the problems are complex, that it is necessary to listen again and learn much from what anyone confronted by these difficulties actually does. The field is open.

A policy of not-judging

By quite a different approach, Eric Fassin's remarks also bring freedom. He confronts us with the fact that, among us, Christians are no longer recognized as the purveyors of norms. In fact the rules and points of reference in

Western societies are no longer grounded in a religious tradition. That has come about first of all in the political system: the will of the people has become the origin of laws and little by little it has been necessary, over the long term, to investigate how this reversal has taken place.

However, that does not mean that for sexuality today – and Eric Fassin returns to the issue several times – there are no longer prohibitions; rather, the churches are no longer asked to define them. The churches can express their positions, formulate criticism, contribute to the debate, and they do so, often in a relevant way, in the spheres of politics, social life, the economy, education and culture. Where this transfer has not been accomplished is in the realm of life, from conception to death: the status of the embryo, stem cells, abortion, sex education, how a couple lives and what form the couple takes, birth control, sexual regimes, extending as far as euthanasia and the right to arrange one's death.

Here is a hypothesis to consider calmly: when we come to what affects human life and sexuality we are in the last stage of this disappropriation. Since society always has to take decisions in these spheres, it will be interested in hearing a word nourished by Christian traditions, but that will no longer be seen to decree what must or must not be done – moreover such a course would presuppose still having more or less the same means of making these definitions respected.

Some people feel nostalgic about these tasks and the powers which have been lost. I prefer to rejoice, since I see here an opportunity for life according to the gospel. Freed from a task which has become impossible, Christian energies have become available for other missions. Let's reflect that when we are no longer caught up in the logic of permission and prohibition, what we say will be freer and its spiritual potential will be able to deploy itself anew. What we say will be available for and capable of being made fruitful in all situations, without claiming to itself the right, let alone the duty, to judge.

That renews the question of 'non-judgement'. You have read in this book that this was the first of the positions formulated by the association. This attitude had been vigorously formulated by the English Christians who preceded us in the struggle against AIDS during the 1980s: 'To be non-judgemental' was the order of the day. Now we are called on to extend this requirement in relations with individuals to the collective sphere. Not judging is a political attitude in the broad sense of the term: that isn't often said.

Words for living

Sexuality concerns the whole of the life of the sexual beings that we are. Thinking must advance beyond a necessary morality which promotes norms, obligations and prohibitions, along the lines of an ethic. According to Paul Ricoeur, let us listen to 'what allows us to conjure up the extreme fragility of the human condition' or again 'what teaches us to be free'. So we need values and meaning. Timothy Radcliffe has suggested some values as a basis for a 'Christian sexual ethic'. Certainly this is not an ethic reserved for Christians, which could be presented as a norm. Can one perhaps speak of a Christian contribution to an ethic of sexuality?

The values which help us to live a good and just life will not necessarily be new. Sometimes we will have to articulate them in a different way and open them to situations which hitherto have been neglected. Here are two examples.

Fidelity is recognized as a virtue if it is engaged in until death in the framework of marriage. But what if it were thought of, more broadly, as everything that manifests the strength of a bond of love over a long period? Isn't it possible to live that out also, even if it doesn't last a whole lifetime or even if it translates into what a number of young people call 'successive fidelities'? What if fidelity could be welcomed in every couple who love, within or outside marriage, and also when it is not between a man and a woman? In fact today fidelity is wanted and experienced in other forms and new rhythms. It isn't nothing. Let's not be afraid to recognize some explosion of its beauty in new forms of this virtue.

Some live out chastity in the joy of a spiritual commitment. Many others see it as austere mastery of the desires and a sorry relationship to the body. We need to recall that contrary to the media use of this word, it isn't identified with continence. It is offered to everyone by the Christian tradition: 'Chaste spouses' was the title of a 1931 encyclical. What if its force were rediscovered as the virtue of pleasure and the respect which flows from wonderment at the other and oneself when desire takes form? Then it could give rise to the right attitudes. Couldn't one then speak of chastity without fear, and to everyone, in order to put some meaning into existence?

In passing, another value arises: respect, for oneself and the other. It would be easy to find the basis for respect in the gospel, but that has hardly been developed by Christianity. This book has mentioned respect in passing here and there; only the chapter 'Positions and Questions' has emphasized it. In these times which seem so hard, respect sheds light on the right way of practising sexuality. That isn't self-evident. In a class where means of prevention were being taught, pupils said, 'Respect? No one has ever spoken to us about that.' To talk of respect is also to recall that an ethic of sexuality can reject whatever damages human beings.

So to hold, sometimes to renew, convictions dear to Christians could be to shed some light on what the French surrealist André Breton called the 'unbreakable kernel of night' in sexuality. The attempt will always have its limits. Happily, there are words which help us to live. Christians, those who follow the gospel, have and will have more to say, not in order to damage, imprison or kill but in order to support, affirm, give meaning. Like the Word on which it is based, an authentic Christian word is a word which saves.

The book ends here. Like all books, it is only words on paper, handed on to its readers. The hope of those who have written it is that these pages don't remain a dead letter, that they are taken in, discussed, criticized, extended, overtaken, and that readers may perhaps find life in this movement. Then hope is born, the virtue cherished by every Christian.

Contributors

Lytta Basset is Swiss. A psychoanalyst, philosopher and Protestant theologian, she has been a pastor in Geneva. She taught theology at the University of Lausanne and now teaches in Neuchâtel. She is editor of the journal *La Chair et le Souffle*, founded in 2005. Her publications include *Guérir du malheur*, Albin Michel 1999; *La Joie impregnable*, Albin Michel 2004; and *Sainte colère, Jacob, Job, Jésus*, Bayard 2002.

Eric Fassin is a sociologist. He teaches at the École normale superieure in Paris, where he holds a seminar entitled 'Sexuality today. The policy and knowledge of the genre, of sexuality and filiation'. His recent publications include *Liberté, égalite, sexualités* (with Clarisse Fabre), editions 10.18 2004; *L'inversion de la question homosexuelle*, Éditions Amsterdam 2005; *De la question sociale á la question raciale? Représenter la société française* (edited, with Didier Fassin), La Découverte 2006.

Abdon Goudjo is a doctor of public health. He works

with CRIPS (Regional Centres for Information about and Prevention of AIDS) in Paris. He co-ordinates programmes against HIV/AIDS in the Congo for the French Ministry of Foreign Affairs.

Antoine Lion, a Dominican living in Paris, is the founder of the 'Christians & AIDS' association.

Timothy Radcliffe is a Dominican. He lives at Blackfriars in Oxford, where he has taught biblical theology. From 1992 to 2001 he was Master of the Order of Preachers. Since then he has preached and lectured in many countries. His books include *I Call you Friends*, Continuum 2003; *Seven Last Words*, Continuum 2004; *What is the Point of Being a Christian?*, Continuum 2005.

Jean-Louis Vildé is President of the 'Christians & AIDS' association.

'Chrétiens & sida', 30 rue Boucry, 75018 Paris. www.chretiens-sida.com

—